SKIMPY

SKIMPY

OUTRAGEOUS TRUE TALES OF CROCS, SNAKES & PULLING BEERS IN THE TOP END

KELLIE ARROWSMITH

hachette AUSTRALIA

Some pseudonyms have been used in this book and other details altered where necessary to protect the identity and privacy of people mentioned.

 hachette
AUSTRALIA

Published in Australia and New Zealand in 2015
by Hachette Australia
(an imprint of Hachette Australia Pty Limited)
Level 17, 207 Kent Street, Sydney NSW 2000
www.hachette.com.au

10 9 8 7 6 5 4 3 2 1

National Library of Australia
Cataloguing-in-Publication data:

Arrowsmith, Kellie, author.

Skimpy: outrageous true tales of crocs, snakes and pulling beers
in the top end/Kellie Arrowsmith.

ISBN 978 073363 438 3 (paperback)

Arrowsmith, Kellie.
Arrowsmith, Kellie – Humor.
Women – Northern Territory – Biography.
Country life – Northern Territory – Biography.
Northern Territory – Description and travel.

920.720994

Cover design by Luke Causby, Blue Cork Design
Landscape photograph courtesy of Luke Causby
Author photograph courtesy of Danial Gowans, danialgowans.com
Text design by Blue Cork Design
Typeset in Garamond by Kirby Jones
Printed and bound in Australia by Griffin Press, Adelaide, an accredited
ISO AS/NZS 14001:2009 Environmental Management System printer

The paper this book is printed on is certified against the Forest Stewardship Council® Standards. Griffin Press holds FSC chain of custody certification SGS-COC-005088. FSC promotes environmentally responsible, socially beneficial and economically viable management of the world's forests.

In memory of Elsie and Barb, my angels
— I know you're up there, cheering me on.

CONTENTS

CHAPTER 1

GETTING TO THE GOLD COAST

RAISING A MINER'S HARD HAT ABOVE MY head, I pushed my way through the crowded bar of the rough old bush pub, dressed – if you could call it that – in a sexy little schoolgirl outfit. If I'd worn this when I actually was at high school, I would've ended up expelled or pregnant.

'Support your local skimpy!' I called out to the crowd of mine workers, encouraging them to pull some cash from their pockets and put it into the hat I'd borrowed from one of them.

A couple of blokes dressed in office suits tried to avoid my gaze, suddenly finding the labels on their beer bottles extremely interesting. Luckily for me, I had insured myself in the form of a brawny bauxite miner who had a shitload of tattoos and no brains. I'd fed the bloke double rums all night, at cost price, so now I was his favourite person, which was unfortunate for the nerdy-looking accountant types who'd just given me the cold shoulder.

'What the fuck's wrong with you wankers? Put some money in the hat, ya fuckin' tight-arses!' my hero, who'd just flown in from Western Australia, roared at them. The suits reluctantly took out their wallets and scrounged around for a few coins.

'What the fuck? Put ya change away and give the lady a proper tip!' The rowdy miner reached across, grabbed a twenty-dollar note out of one poor bloke's wallet and threw it in the hat I was holding. 'There,' he announced to the suit, who was now well and truly shitting himself. 'That's how you tip the girls!'

It was February 2011 and I'd recently arrived in Gove, which rhymes with 'stove' and is also known as Nhulunbuy, a tiny community on the east side of Arnhem Land in the Northern Territory. The Walkabout Tavern, where I'd started working, is the heart and soul of this isolated mining town.

Gove is the largest town in Arnhem Land, with a pub, club, golf course, swimming pool and Woolworths. The locals were a mix of miners' families and the Aboriginal community that owned the land. Situated in the top end of Australia, for six months of the year Gove is surrounded by croc-infested floodwaters, making it virtually impossible to get in or out by road. During this time, food, petrol and other supplies arrived by barge or plane.

So how did a girl from country Victoria get here? Believe me, I'd asked myself the same question …

In the late 1980s I'd grown up in a country town called Rosedale, located on the Princes Highway in Gippsland, Victoria. The town boasted a population of about 1500 when I was there, although these days I think it's around the 3000 to 4000 mark. And, I've been told, it even has a traffic light now.

Living in Rosedale as a kid was awesome. Surrounded by dairy farms and forestry, it was the kind of place where you could spend the whole day riding your bike around with your mates and your parents would never worry. I was lucky enough to grow up riding horses – or unlucky, depending on how you look at it. The number of times I was nearly killed by a horse was ridiculous. My mate Melissa and I both owned highly strung ex-racehorses. One time we decided to go for a bit of a gallop along a grassy laneway, about three kilometres out of town, but things soon got out of our control.

Both our horses were naturally competitive, so when Melissa's horse bolted past me without Melissa on its back, I knew I was in huge trouble. Trying unsuccessfully to stop my horse, I decided the safest thing to do was abandon ship, so I threw myself off as eight hooves pounded past. After rolling around on the ground, the wind knocked out of me, I finally got up and saw Melissa walking towards me, looking as dishevelled as I felt.

We looked at each other and started laughing, probably slightly hysterically. We laughed the whole way up the road as we watched our horses disappear into the distance. By the time we got to the nearest house to ask for help we were in tears, we'd laughed that much. We composed ourselves enough to knock on the door and ask for help. We got a lift back to the horse paddock and, to our surprise, there were our horses, standing at the gate. Also waiting for us were the local fire brigade, the police, and an ambulance that I'm guessing had come from the next town, because Rosedale didn't have a hospital. I'm pretty sure they weren't laughing.

Melissa lived in an older-style house with a picket fence out the front. One day we returned from riding as her mum was in the hallway talking on the phone. I tied my horse by the reins to the picket fence. It's a big no-no to tie up your horse by the reins but my horse was really quiet, so I thought, she'll be right. You also shouldn't tie them up to picket fences, but I tied her to that fence anyway.

SKIMPY

It turned out my horse was only quiet up to a point, because something happened and she got a fright. As she jumped back, ten metres' worth of fence line went with her. And as she took off down the road, pretty much the entire fence dragged behind her. So I ran after her, grabbed her and the fence, and dragged them both back.

Melissa and I propped up the fence. Melissa's mum was still on the phone and she didn't see a thing, even though the front door opened straight onto the yard. About a week later Melissa's brother was leaning on the fence – it fell over and he got in so much trouble for it. We didn't bother to get him out of trouble, of course. We used to join in the fun when the boys would do something to piss off their mum – like throwing fruit at a ceiling fan when it was on high speed or the time we decided to mix every ingredient in the pantry into one gigantic vomit-looking mess on the kitchen bench – and then got the hell out of there before the boys stopped doing it so they'd get in trouble for it. I didn't have older brothers, so it was great to terrorise someone else's.

Horse riding set me up pretty well for later life, too. If you can handle a horse you can handle pretty much anything life throws at you, because handling half a tonne of pony at the age of eight is no mean feat. But the only time I was ever really scared of a horse was when Mum bought me an evil

7

spotty mare named Becky, who I swear was out to kill me – and nearly succeeded a few times! That's how much I loved riding. I'd rather ride the Devil Pony than no pony at all.

Horses aside, highlights of living in Rosedale as a teenager basically consisted of the local milk bar – where we could buy both lollies *and* cigarettes – and the Roadhouse, which my mother banned me from hanging out at. This just made the seedy truck stop even more appealing, especially because that's where all the older kids hung out, drinking coffee and smoking, telling us about all the things we had to look forward to, like drinking goon out of a cask outside the blue-light disco, hooking up with boys and – my favourite – throwing up all over your mate's parents' house. (I never did this myself, although when I was fourteen I kind of redecorated my mate's mum's car – but, to be fair, I'd had three-quarters of a bottle of Wipeout and that shit is nasty.)

When I was fourteen, Mum and Dad split up and Mum moved us kids up to Albury to live with her new partner, Brendon. Our move to a new town coincided with me reaching the age when I wanted to try new things. And I guess when you move to a new place you kind of want to fit in. I wasn't sporty and I wasn't a nerd. The only place I really fitted in was with the kids who smoked and wagged school and did all the bad-arse shit I thought was cool. In primary school I'd pretty much been a goody two-shoes. I did all the assignments on time and did what the teacher said and all that sort of stuff. I remember one of the rare times I was sent to the principal's office I carried on like I was walking the green mile. I was devastated to be in the bad books. But once I was in high school – from the time I was fourteen – I hung out with all the smokers on the oval and we just wagged school all the time. Mum reckons that she spent more time at the school in Year Eleven than I did.

I remember one time we had a substitute teacher in legal studies; his name was Mr O'Shaughnessy and he was about a hundred years old. And he was deaf and pretty much blind – he was so bloody old he had no senses left. My friend and I were sitting together in the class, saying to each other, 'Geez, why didn't we wag?' If we'd known it was Mr O'Shaughnessy we wouldn't have shown up to class.

'You go to the toilet,' I said to my friend, 'and I'll meet you at the shop.'

So my friend went to the bathroom, and when Mr O'Shaughnessy turned around to write something on the blackboard, I jumped out the window and went off to meet her at the shop. So that was pretty much me in high school.

My sister is four years younger than me, and my brother younger than that again, and at that point in your life four years is a big difference. I wasn't interested in my brother and sister. I was very self-absorbed, as most teenage girls are – I was just interested in me and my friends and I didn't really hang out with my siblings much. They were just too young. My sister was into the Spice Girls and I was into Nirvana. That was a major point of difference, as anyone who grew up in the late nineties would know. We had nothing in common at that point apart from bloodlines and living arrangements.

When it came to schoolwork I only chose to do what I wanted to do. I was so interested in history that I came top of the class in one test – I remember one of the really nerdy kids cracked it when I got a higher mark than her in the test. She reckoned it was bullshit because I never showed up to any other classes. But I really loved history. I just loved stories – especially true stories. If something really happened it's a lot more interesting to me than something that's been made up. Especially Australian history and the Ancient Egyptians – I loved them. But otherwise, if I didn't like it, once I got old enough to say, 'Bugger it, I'm not going', I didn't go.

Once I was sixteen, there was no way in hell you would catch me hanging out at truck stops and shopping centres like I did at fourteen. By that stage they had banned indoor smoking and, besides, I was too busy trying not to get kicked out of the local nightclub. The head bouncer happened to be

Australia's own Derek Boyer (of *Housos* fame), but back then he spent his nights either refusing me entry or finding me hiding in a dark corner of the club and marching me down the stairs. When I finally turned eighteen I ended up working at the same pub as him, but he still liked to cut me off from the bar if he thought I was getting out of control. Which I was, more often than not.

I'd still make the trip from Albury to Rosedale to visit my mates, but because the Roadhouse had gone all anti-smoking we started sneaking into one of the two local pubs. The pub had been taken over by a bloke from out of town, so he didn't really give a shit how old we were, as long as we kept buying drinks. We would usually sit out the back with the jukebox, leaving the front bar to the old blokes. One particular drunken night we were up to our usual teenage shenanigans out the back when I heard one of the boys, who was ordering drinks at the bar, shout out, 'There's a fuckin' horse in the bar!' Thinking he had clearly had too much to drink, we laughed at him then went back to our drinks ... until I looked through the doorway into the front bar and saw that there *was* a horse in the pub. And he looked pretty bloody thirsty.

Growing up in Rosedale was a great character-building experience for all of us lucky enough to be there. If anything, it made us all work hard, so that when we were old enough we could get the fuck out of there! Most of us ended up in Queensland – but before that stage I had a few years in Albury.

Albury is a large country town on the New South Wales/ Victoria border, with the Murray River separating it from the Victorian town of Wodonga (or, as I like to call it, The Shithole). I had my own little flat in East Albury, located two blocks from the main street, which meant I had no need for a car. I worked as a plumber's labourer for an old bloke called Tinky, who was loads of fun to work for because getting drunk with him at the local pub was part of my job description. And living around the corner from Mum had its advantages. For instance, if I wanted a nice home-cooked meal I only had to walk two blocks (actually, Mum wasn't the one cooking – my stepdad is the masterchef in that house). As much as my mother and I love each other, living together at that point of my life was impossible. That was probably more my fault than hers, though. As a teenager I was a total bitch, especially if someone tried to tell me 'no'. Obviously that didn't go down too well with either of my parents, so moving out of home to live in a unit down the road was the best option. Mum still felt like she could keep an eye on me while giving me the freedom I craved.

Despite this freedom, though, and despite a great boss and permission to drink on the job, I was getting bored. I didn't want to be digging holes and fixing toilets for the rest of my days. There had to be more to life than that.

So when an old school friend invited me to share a unit with him on the Gold Coast, I jumped at the chance. I told Mum I was moving to Queensland to 'find myself', which is another way of saying I had no fucking clue what I was doing with my life. She was understandably upset – how the hell would she keep an eye on me if I was living interstate?

CHAPTER 2

GOLD CHAINS AND BOTOX

LIKE MANY PEOPLE IN THEIR EARLY twenties, I was under the impression that the Gold Coast was *the* place to be and, for the most part, I wasn't wrong. Waterfront restaurants and high-end boutiques are flanked by golden beaches and lush rainforest. Pacific Fair, one of Australia's largest shopping centres, is located in the heart of Broadbeach, a suburb not far from where I lived. I had a love–hate relationship with Pacific Fair. I longed for all the shiny new stuff displayed in the fancy boutiques but could never afford to buy any of it.

Soon after my arrival, the old school friend who'd convinced me to move up to the Coast had charmed his way into my heart – and my pants.

Shaun and I had grown up in Rosedale together and known each other since we were about five years old. As teenagers we had 'hooked up' on a few occasions, and when he suggested I move to the Gold Coast I kind of had an idea that we might hook up again. It wasn't my intention to settle down, though, as I had plans to save some money and keep travelling north. In the meantime I saw no harm in having a bit of fun together. Back then I thought he was pretty hot, with his blond highlights, big blue eyes and tribal tatts. But I didn't have any idea what I wanted in a bloke and I soon learnt you *should* sometimes judge a book by its cover. Or, in other words, if a bloke spends more time and money highlighting his hair than you do, the relationship is probably not meant to be.

Within a couple of days of my arrival on the Gold Coast I'd had to find a job, because life on the Glitter Strip isn't cheap. I applied for anything that was advertised and hit the local shops to beg for work. I soon scored a job working for $12 an hour behind the counter of the carvery at The Pines shopping centre. It was one of the most depressing jobs ever. The youngest person working there – apart from me – was around sixty-five years old. Which was not surprising, considering most of our customers came from the aged care home up the road. I ended up volunteering to be the 'dishpig' just so I could hang out at the back of the shop, listening to the radio and avoiding conversations about arthritis and the price of bananas.

After six months of living together in a share house with another bloke, Shaun and I moved into a canal-side unit and a more serious relationship. For the first few months, living together was great. We made good use of the barbecue, chilling on our bedroom balcony and pretending to be rich because we lived next to a tiny bit of water. I tried my luck fishing from the canal, which was full of bream, but I usually ended up getting the line stuck in the neighbours' fence. Since then I've had many opportunities to master the art of fishing, but I've never managed to do it. Or enjoy it, for that matter.

At the start, Shaun wanted the house, the kids and the white picket fence more than I did. He was training six days a week at a Muay Thai gym and working hard as a renderer. After a year he had saved up enough money for us to move into a house, which he had bought with his parents, in Palm Beach.

By this stage I had warmed to the idea of settling into a family life but it was now too late for Shaun: the bright lights and temptations of the underworld seemed to have taken priority over his earlier goals, and it was at this point that I started my three-year relationship with easyroommate.com, moving back and forth between the home I shared with Shaun and living with strangers in share houses.

Shaun and I had some legendary fights. I remember arguing in his car (Shaun's pride and joy was a hotted-up Commodore with tinted windows) and being pissed off about something he'd said and on my high horse until we pulled into the driveway. I slammed the car door shut – so hard it shattered the window. I went from wanting to kill Shaun to fearing for my own life and quickly ran up the road to a mate's house, where I hid out until I thought it was safe to go home. That cost me $80 and a week's worth of doing the dishes.

The funniest argument we ever had (well, funny for me, anyway) was the night he went out and said he'd be back by around 10 p.m. When he finally showed up, at 9.30 the next morning, he found his bed, wardrobe and toothbrush on the front lawn (my plan was to sleep on the queen-size bed in the spare room). I blame my temper on both my Irish background and the fact that Shaun had a funny relationship with the truth. I didn't stay mad for too long, though, especially since I got to watch him carry his bedroom furniture back up the stairs with a raging hangover and no sleep. That cheered me right up.

After living in a country town that boasted the local river, the weir and the pub as major forms of entertainment, I was in heaven up there with the theme parks, festivals and markets. There was every type of hobby or sport you could think of. I tried everything from pole dancing to Bikram yoga. (If you have no idea what Bikram yoga is, it involves twisting into ridiculous positions in a poky little room heated to forty degrees with about thirty other people who are also inhaling their own sweat.) I even attended a hula-hooping class. But after an hour of watching a crazy hippie lady show me every which way I could swing a hula hoop, I figured there wasn't much more I needed to learn, especially since she was selling the bloody things so I could just buy one to take home and save myself twenty bucks an hour. I still have the hula hoop. It's currently in the corner of my spare bedroom, gathering dust alongside the stripper pole, the Ab King Pro and a yoga mat.

There's a fairly large number of over-sixties living on the Gold Coast (although by the way half of the elderly population carried on, you wouldn't think so). When I first arrived I'd go to the local beach and see wrinkled, old leather-skinned men and women covered in gold jewellery and fading tattoos. There'd be old women sunbaking topless with boobs that resembled fried eggs hanging out and, lying beside them, mahogany-skinned old men wearing nothing but gold chains and Speedos.

The finest example of mutton dressed as lamb I have ever witnessed worked at the fish and chip shop up the road. You would see this woman in the supermarket and from behind she looked like Paris Hilton (this was around the time Paris Hilton was cool and she used to wear those cargo miniskirts and little tight tank tops), then she'd turn around and it was like a scene from a horror movie. She had to be at least sixty, although she was obviously in denial about this. And if that made her happy, good for her. I personally can't wait to get to the age when it's acceptable to go shopping in clothes that resemble pyjamas, and take naps in the middle of the day.

It wasn't just the over-sixty crowd that drew attention to themselves every time they went out in public. Because the Coast is one of Australia's biggest holiday destinations, it has become the number one spot to find the nation's biggest tools. The males of the species usually have the following features: identical tribal tattoos, chunky gold chains, Ed Hardy shirts, thick, steroid-enhanced bodies, and bumbags. Yep, bumbags. Someone told them bumbags are cool and they believed it. The females usually wear fake eyelashes, hair extensions and stage make-up even if they're only going as far as the local supermarket. If you've ever seen an episode of *Jersey Shore* you'll know instantly what I'm on about. These girls make Snooki look like a natural beauty.

The first few years I lived on the Gold Coast I stayed true to my word and spent my spare time 'finding myself'.

But it can brainwash anyone. Even I started buying into the bullshit after a while. Growing up in a country town,

I'd always been outside, riding horses and getting dirty. To me a 'hairstyle' meant I'd brushed it and pulled it back into a ponytail. On the rare occasion I'd had acrylic nails my mother commented that I should get them done all the time because they hid the dirt. I guess I've just always had better things to do with my time than file my nails. Yet suddenly here I was googling boob jobs and Botox, even though I had no money and was only in my mid-twenties. On the Gold Coast, Botox and Restylane injections are as normal as getting a haircut. I knew a few girls who were getting regular Botox injections at the age of twenty-one. I didn't succumb to it and, looking back, I think it probably would have been a waste of time and money. I'm in my thirties now, and for someone who smoked and drank her way through her twenties, I don't reckon I'm doing too bad. Bigger boobs would be nice but, then again, so would a trip around the world, and I can't afford that either.

If I needed anything done, it was a brain transplant so I would see the light and leave the toxic relationship with my boyfriend. Shaun and I had turned into *that* couple – you know, the one that you wish would either get married or kill each other and be done with it. At first, the fights were over as quickly as they'd started and making up was half the fun, but it soon became obvious that we wanted different things out of life. I reckon it had something to do with it being our first adult relationship yet we were still acting like adolescents.

The end was definitely coming, that was for sure. After six years together I was bored with sitting in the backyard drinking every weekend. The most excitement was when someone turned up with a bag of coke or a few pills. Shaun's days as a health freak, training six days a week at the local kickboxing gym, were well and truly over. Since he'd decided to try his hand at selling all sorts of substances that weren't exactly legal, he'd ended up with a cocaine addiction and caused a major car crash on the M1.

I'd started to seriously question what the fuck we were doing together. Apart from smoking a bit of weed, I had no interest in the seedy world of drugs and nightclubs. What I fantasised about was buying a bus and driving around Australia. For two years I'd lived in a share house with backpackers from different countries who had seen more of Australia than I had. I spent many nights listening to their amazing stories about travelling through the outback, seeing Uluru and snorkelling around the Great Barrier Reef, and wondered when I would get to do it all myself.

But first, I needed a change of career.

CHAPTER 3

THE TOY SHOW

'KATY, I JUST GOT AN EMAIL FROM YOUR 7 p.m. show in Brisbane last night … apparently he thought the show was okay but he wrote – and I quote – "The stripper wasn't very articulate and didn't seem to want to have a conversation after her show." Sorry, I was told to pass on the feedback.'

'Not articulate enough? I'm a stripper, not a politician. I'm paid to dance naked not give a speech, for fuck's sake! What the hell does he expect?'

I had to admit, she had a good point.

As well as an unstable relationship, unfulfilled travel plans and the drama of having to live with total strangers from easyroommate.com every time my boyfriend and I took a 'break', I also experimented with a series of different 'careers'.

As I tried to find one I actually liked, my jobs ranged from embarrassing to downright dodgy. After giving the carvery the arse, I found work with a lady who ran a garden maintenance company in Sanctuary Cove, a gated community where the cheapest house is about a million dollars. It wasn't much fun, though, getting stabbed in the eye by cycads in someone's front yard for a measly ten bucks an hour as the owners pulled out of their driveway in a brand new Lexus. I gave up that job after I realised I was spending half my pay on Lotto tickets in the hope that I could move to Sanctuary Cove myself.

I moved on to work as a bottle shop attendant, thinking my enthusiastic attitude towards alcohol would see me running the place in no time. Instead, I ended up working in a drive-thru across from the local methadone clinic. For a while, apart from my workmates, the only real conversations I engaged in were with the local drug addicts, which was good practice for when my boyfriend decided to try his luck as an entrepreneur in the booming meth industry that was taking over the country at the time.

Next I scored an office junior role at a dating agency. But it wasn't long before I realised that the objective of this company was to rip-off lonely people from small rural towns. When I discovered that a client had lost his house trying to pay the fees this agency was charging him, I made a few anonymous calls to some government departments and got the fuck out of there. (They are now closed down and being dealt with by the courts.) After two more years of data entry – not a great career choice for someone who has the attention span of a goldfish – a former housemate got me a job working as a receptionist for one of the Gold Coast's biggest stripping agencies.

I'd never really known much about this industry until I'd moved into a large share house in Mudgeeraba. One of the girls who lived with me, Katy, was a stripper and worked for the agency. Before I met her I had no idea that strippers didn't just work in strip clubs. In fact, I soon learnt that that was a crap way to make money, and that private parties such as bucks' nights were where the money was at. Whereas in a strip club the girls sometimes have to pay a fee to be there and hustle all night giving lap dances for $50 a pop, the private shows paid up to $500 for half an hour, depending on just how raunchy you were prepared to go. Spending a couple of nights tagging along while Katy was working was an eye-opener, to say the least.

The agency sent girls to pubs all over the Gold Coast and Brisbane, as well as Kalgoorlie in Western Australia and Gove in the Northern Territory, to work as topless waitresses or 'skimpy barmaids'. 'Skimpy' is a nickname for the girls who work behind the bar dressed in a cheeky outfit, such as a nurse or schoolgirl, and strip down to lingerie or a bikini after passing a jug around the bar for tips. This work is mainly done in mining towns, although a few bars on the Gold Coast and in Brisbane run on the same principle, except the girls wear lingerie then go topless halfway through their shifts for tips.

The agency also booked out showgirls for bucks' nights, birthdays and pretty much any time a group of blokes could find a half-arsed excuse to hire a stripper.

Geez, could these girls put on a show. The things some of them could do with a Chupa Chup and a banana were incredible! People might assume that anyone can be a stripper and it's easy, but I can assure you that most of the girls I saw perform were either gymnasts or acrobats or they did a lot of ballet growing up. Another assumption many people make is that strippers are uneducated/drug addicts/prostitutes. Okay, yes, this is true in some cases, but most of the girls I met were studying, or raising children and trying to provide for them. One showgirl who was the best dancer I have ever seen had a double degree in chemistry. So there really isn't a stereotype; like any other industry, it takes all kinds.

Apart from getting to watch the occasional strip show for free when one of the girls was stuck and needed a driver (if I was a bloke I would have been in heaven), I chatted on the phone to strange men about what specifically was involved in a Fruit and Veg duo. Don't even get me started on the Big Greek Salad. After seeing that particular show, let's just say I've never been able to eat one again. It took a few weeks before I was able to rattle off the ins and outs of different shows to the customers without putting my hand over the phone and asking whoever was working with me, 'What the fuck is involved in a Bubble Bath show, anyway? Do they bring a plastic pool or do they do the show in the bathroom?!' I was given a list of shows and their descriptions, but sometimes even the descriptions baffled me – phrases like 'open leg work' and 'double penetration' (yes, that sounds straightforward but when you're talking about a lesbian show it can get confusing).

After the customer chose the type of show they wanted they would request the girl they wanted to perform the show. Of course they didn't always get who they wanted, but as I used to say to them, you're ordering a person, not a pizza. We also booked out topless waitress and promo girls, so to say I was flat out in the office most of the time would be an understatement.

My boss was a tiny little woman with dark hair, olive skin and a huge personality. The best way to describe her would be to say she was like Eddie off *Absolutely Fabulous*. A complete contradiction of herself at the best of times, she was into crystal healing and vegetarian food but could also party harder than most people half her age. It wasn't unusual for me to rock up to work in the morning and find twenty people still partying from the night before in the pool area outside the office. Those days were often both interesting and unproductive as half-pissed visitors randomly popped into the office to have a chat while I was attempting to work. Describing sex shows to strange men over the phone is hard enough without having people shouting out smart-arse comments and laughing in the background.

Announcing to me on the first day I came to work for her that she was never having children because 'she couldn't think of anything more boring', my boss sponsored World Vision kids and guide dogs. I suppose the way she looked at it was that instead of adding to the world's problems she'd rather help fix them. Plus, you can sponsor kids without having to hang out with them.

I got along with her most of the time, but it could be frustrating working in that environment. I'd usually be in the office, calmly getting on with my day's work, and then my boss would burst in and completely mind-boggle me, firing off instructions and questions at a million miles an hour without waiting for a response: 'Okay, honey, have you sent out the addresses for this weekend's jobs? Who's booked into Moss

Street today? Have you confirmed all the pubs yet? What do you mean Candy didn't show up for her shift? Well, why didn't you replace her? There's heaps of girls available. Why don't you swap Bubbles and Amy into this pub and we'll get Bambi to replace Candy? Geez, it's not rocket science, babe. Why is this girl booked in at Rocklea? She was there last week. I need you to swap this girl over to this job because we double-booked that shift; we can't have them both turning up. Have you sent out the date and times for next week's photo shoot? I need you to drop a promo pack off to these guys on your way home. Oh, and get the mail on your way in tomorrow morning. Can you take the phone home with you tonight, babe? I'm going out for dinner. Oh, and text Candy and tell her she's fined $50 for the no-show and if she does it one more time she's sacked.' And on it would go, with me frantically trying to write down the instructions as quickly as she fired them off. Then she'd be gone, and I'd be left sitting in my chair feeling like a hurricane had just swept through the office.

Working there was a bit like the relationship with my boyfriend. On any given day it would turn to shit and I'd end up driving home in tears. Girls would cancel jobs at the last minute, expecting me to pull a replacement out of thin air. At the same time I'd have both phones ringing with customers, girls texting the phones to ask me to call pubs or clients because they were running late, then my boss would come in wanting an update while I was talking on one phone, texting on another and with my spare hand trying to type a reply to a client who had decided that requesting a girl via email at 4 p.m. on a Saturday was a great idea. Sometimes it took the patience of a saint coupled with the hide of a rhinoceros to work in that office.

I took the work phone home with me occasionally and sometimes it would ring in the most inappropriate situations. One night it rang during a visit from a girlfriend and her two young children. When I was halfway through booking a thirty-minute 'toy show' for some blokes, my friend's little girl turned to her mum and said, 'Mummy, I want a toy show!' Her little boy then joined in. 'Yeah, Mum, why can't we have a toy show? Pleeeeaaase?'

If you're not already in the know, a toy show involves the type of toys meant for adults, not children. Needless to say, my friend wasn't impressed, and after that she banned me from hanging out with her while I was working.

Sometimes when I described shows on the phone the customers were more gobsmacked than I was, because soon it was just second nature to rattle them off. But after a while, not only was I used to describing what the shows involved, I was getting pretty sick of it. You could tell when guys didn't actually want a stripper, they just wanted to hear you talk about girls playing with sex toys so they could get their rocks off. Guys would ring up and not say anything apart from 'What are you wearing?' My response was usually: 'My pyjamas.' Or sometimes they would ring up drunk, mainly on a Saturday night, just wanting to chat with me like I was some helpline for drunken horny men. I wasn't getting paid enough for *that*. I basically just wanted to tell them to fuck off. In the end, if I had to take the phones on a Saturday night, I made sure there was wine in the fridge.

Once I got the hang of things, I could see that some of the men who booked girls with us had a lot of pressure on them. If they were booking a bucks' night, for example, there was pressure to make the night good for the buck. Boys take their bucks' nights really seriously. Some of them have it planned right down to the last detail and they just want their mate to have a good time. I thought it was cute when they rang up to book some girls and, obviously excited about the whole event, told me unnecessary information about the day (such as what they were planning to cook on the barbie and that they would be going paintballing beforehand and going out to a club later that night) when really all I needed was an address and time that they wanted the show or the waitress.

It was usually the businessmen in the penthouses who were the real pricks. If they had a lot of money, were a little bit older and were 'someone' in society, they were usually a fucking nightmare to deal with. And because they were 'buying' girls – they were paying for them to be there – they just thought the girls were objects, and that used to drive me nuts. The worst offenders were arrogant more than sleazy, and I started to get impatient with the ones who would ring up and be difficult about things. They were paying the exact same amount of money as that 22-year-old guy who had organised a bucks' night for his mate, who had saved up for months with his friends to get that party going, but this dickhead thought he could treat me and the girls like shit just because he had a bit of money. The young guys on the bucks' nights would say 'please' and 'thank you' and 'oh my god I'm so grateful' and then I got some guy who was spending the same amount of money per girl thinking he was better than anyone else because he was richer. I much preferred dealing with the 22-year-old guy who was grateful for my help. It was the Gold Coast, though, so dickheads with too much money and no manners were unavoidable.

There were only a couple of times when jobs went wrong. The first time was actually really funny – the clients rang up and said, 'The stripper's not here any more. She came in and she went to the bathroom and now she's gone.' Then the stripper sent me a text saying, *I quit. This is bullshit. You sent me into a satanic cult ritual party.* I got back in touch with the customers and asked them what the hell was going on and they said, 'We just had some incense and candles burning.' And the funniest thing about it was that the stripper had a satanic symbol tattooed on her back.

Another time a friend of mine who was also a waitress rang me from Jupiter's Casino. I'd sent her to the job because I had the phone that night (I actually had the phone pretty much 24/7 and that's when I developed a phobia towards phones in general. I couldn't even use my own phone for a while). So I sent her to this job and then she rang me up to say that the security guards had kicked these guys out of their apartment, that's how wild they were. Apart from the noise complaints, they'd started throwing bottles around, nearly knocking my mate out.

She felt like their mother because they were really young – 'Oh my god, babe,' she said to me, 'they were, like, eighteen years old.' Then she told me she gave them the money back.

'Why did you do that?' I said, because I couldn't believe she would after what had happened.

'Because I didn't do the full job,' she said.

'You had bottles thrown at your head,' I told her. 'I think you earned your money.'

As well as handling the administration side of things I had to interview potential staff. This is not the kind of job where you need a résumé detailing your education and work history – unless you just graduated with a bachelor's in exotic dancing and have references from a strip club owner. All we really cared about was that the girl had a hot body, a pretty face (or at least knew how to use make-up to make herself look pretty) and nice boobs. This last part was a bit awkward for me at first. Making sure the girls had nice boobs meant I needed to see them. This was compulsory after I accidentally sent a girl I'd just hired to a topless bar without realising that after three kids her boobs resembled those of an eighty-year-old woman. It might sound superficial and nasty but that's the way it is in an industry based solely on looks. Besides, if I was overweight and had saggy boobs the last thing I'd want to do is strut half naked around a pub full of blokes. So the words 'show me your boobs' came out of my mouth at least once a week.

I also handed the girls a list of tips on how to keep their bodies in tip-top shape. My boss had written this up, along with a set of rules she called 'The Constitution', when she first started the agency, and I handed these out to all the new girls. The advice included eating a vegetarian diet, cutting back on dairy, working out, and making sure hair, nails and spray tan were always done to perfection. It's bloody lucky the girls made so much money, because if you followed these tips you would look smoking hot but, trust me, they cost hundreds of dollars. And that's before you added regular Botox injections into the mix, which is pretty much standard procedure in that line of work.

It wasn't usually my job to drive the girls around, but as I mentioned sometimes they got stuck and I had to come to the rescue and get them to their job. One stressful Saturday morning the topless waitress originally booked for a pub shift cancelled at the last minute and the only way I could get someone to replace her was to drive the replacement there myself. So that Saturday afternoon I drove for two hours all the way from the southern end of the Gold Coast to Burpengary, which is at the southern end of the Sunshine Coast, so that the waitress could get to her pub shift on time. The girl – who wasn't paying a cent towards the cost of my petrol – would work for two hours and make $250. I, on the other hand, sat in the car park on my phone taking bookings for the grand total of $30.

While I was in the car park, a little thought popped into my head: why the fuck am I sitting here dealing with phone calls from drunk blokes wanting strippers and being paid a measly $15 an hour when I could be in there selling raffle tickets for $125 an hour? It had taken me two years to reach this earth-shattering conclusion. Just like my relationship with my boyfriend, it took me a long time to wake up to the facts of a situation.

I called my mate Katy. 'I've decided to start doing some skimpy work – whaddya think?'

'I've been waiting for you to come to the other side,' Katy laughed.

'How about we book into Gove?' I said. The agency sent two girls every fortnight up to Gove, where they worked in skimpy outfits or lingerie then went topless for tips. The girls made, on average, four to five grand for the fortnight.

'If I'm allowed back there, yeah, for sure.' Katy, a tall, busty blonde, was always getting banned from pubs, mainly because she was nuts. This chick didn't drink but was a complete sugar addict who would dose herself up on grenadine (which is like the crack cocaine of cordial) then hang from the ceiling fans. She was always allowed back within a year or two, though.

While my boss could be a tad on the scary side, when I told her I wanted to step out from behind the desk she supported me 100 per cent. Although she was a bit disappointed she'd have to look for a new receptionist. She sent me on my way with costumes, shoes, advice and a plane ticket. She even paid for me to do my RSA (Responsible Service of Alcohol) certificate, which you can do online in half an hour – I'd need that to work behind the bar. It was August 2010, I was twenty-seven years old and I was now officially working on 'the other side of the fence'. I hoped I had the balls to see it through.

CHAPTER 4

KEL'S GONE BUSH

To TRAVEL TO GOVE, KATY AND I FIRST HAD to get to Cairns, then change planes. That plane to Gove was a sea of orange shirts. The entire passenger group was all these miners, me and Katy. Katy loved to play up to the whole stripper stereotype. She loved miniskirts and crop tops – when I lived with her (and seven other people) she used to walk around the house in just a G-string without a second thought. Not only that, she had the world's biggest boobs and she was very curvy and very tall and she really stuck out, even when she wasn't on a plane among a group of blokes. So when we got on that plane it was quite obvious we were the skimpies. Everyone stared at us as we walked up the aisle of the plane. Katy didn't give a shit but I was thinking, *Oh holy shit – what am I doing?*

Apart from a landing strip, all there is to mark Gove Airport is a tiny building surrounded by red dirt and with not much more to it than a baggage carousel, a little shop and a booking desk. A big bloke with long, curly dark hair and a massive bushy beard greeted us. Katy knew Dave from one of her five previous trips to Gove. In his early thirties, he reminded me of Hagrid out of *Harry Potter* with a bit of late Russell Crowe thrown in. He had that whole you'll-be-safe-with-me-cos-I-wrestle-crocodiles-for-fun aura about him. He had a cheeky grin and a sparkle in his eye that instantly attracted me.

Dave drove us to the pub to pick up the keys to our accommodation. On the way he gave us a little tour. 'There's the G3 camp ... that's where most of the boys from the mine live. They aren't supposed to have anyone stay with them but you always see girls doing the walk of shame at 6 a.m. Well, I assume that's what they're doing, unless they're just going for an early morning walk in a miniskirt and heels ...

'There's the hospital, girls. Yep, only one around for about 1500 kilometres and it's not that flash either ... I mean, it's okay for most things but if you've just cut your arm off, you're pretty much fucked.'

It was around this part of the tour that I started to wonder where the hell I actually was. And what the hell was this 'Arnhem Land' place he kept mentioning? You can imagine how embarrassed I was when I found out that we were actually *in* Arnhem Land. I really didn't pay much attention during geography at school. (For those of you who also have no idea where and what Arnhem Land is, it's traditional Aboriginal land located in the north-east corner of the Northern Territory and the Aboriginal people have lived there for around 40,000 years.)

Never having been to the top of the Northern Territory (or the bottom, for that matter), I did notice the difference in the landscape. It was pretty dark when we first arrived, so all I saw at first was the road into town. On either side of the road was bushland, although the trees didn't seem to be as thick or tall as the gumtrees in the southern part of the country. As we got closer to town the bushland turned into street lights and tropical shrubs. There was rust-coloured dirt everywhere – and I mean *everywhere*. White cars turned a pinkish colour after driving around Gove for a day. And if you went for a walk for longer than five minutes you would be covered in a mixture of sweat and dust. It was the wet season when we arrived, and after leaving the Gold Coast on a cool morning, the humidity that had greeted us when we got off the plane nearly made me pass out.

We pulled up at the Walkabout Tavern, which is on the main street of Gove. The ocean was less than 100 metres from the pub but it wasn't really safe to swim there – apart from crocs, there were stingers and sharks galore.

Scattered along the side of the road were a few palm trees and more red dirt. The pub's car park was packed with mud-caked four-wheel drives and boat trailers. The pub itself was old, rough and dirty with yellow-stained ceilings and electrical cords hanging out of the walls in random places. The bar was crowded with mine workers still in uniform, and one of the girls I knew from the Gold Coast waved at us from behind the bar where she was pouring beers, topless. The whole place smelt of sweat, booze and smoke. I thought it was fucking awesome.

It was around 9 p.m. and, to our surprise, the pub management said they had no idea that we were arriving that night. This was bullshit, because the girls flew up every fortnight. When they said they'd have no beds available for us until the next morning, Dave offered to let us stay with him. I should have been nervous, not knowing this bloke from a bar of soap, but it had been a long day and I was just grateful to have somewhere to stay at all. Besides, Katy seemed to know him quite well and I trusted her judgement (most of the time).

Dave took us to a bush bash in an old outback shed on the outskirts of town that the locals affectionately referred to as the Hog Shed. It was a birthday party for Al, one of Dave's best mates. Half the town was out there celebrating. Gove is partly made up of locals who have lived there permanently for years and do normal jobs like school teacher, nurse and so on. Some locals work in the mines but live in Gove and have houses in town. The rest of the town is made up of FIFO (fly in fly out) workers who work in the mines and have temporary accommodation at the G3 camp. Tonight's crowd was mainly locals.

Dave had lived in town for about eight years, working in the mine at first then scoring a job out bush, grading roads and airstrips for all of the communities in East Arnhem Land. Dave's mate Al, a security guard who had also arrived in Gove a few years earlier and never looked back, was a big Maltese bloke with a personality to match. He was in the middle of the dance floor when we walked in and that's pretty much where he stayed all night.

The band was pumping but anyone who could play an instrument was welcome to get up onstage and join in, and the dance floor was packed. But it was nothing like a dance floor in a Gold Coast club. These people were real, down-to-earth country types and didn't give a rat's arse what they looked like. Everyone was too busy having a good time.

I was amused to find that the loo was a typical outback dunny with corrugated-iron walls. Nothing like the toilets in a Gold Coast nightclub either. For a start, no one was doing lines of coke off the toilet seat.

Dave introduced us to a large group of locals and we sat chatting to them for a while until the alcohol (or red cordial, in Katy's case) kicked in and she and I hit the dance floor. Out the back was a bunch of old blokes puffing on joints, something I could never resist. Before I knew it they were my best buddies and I was as stoned as a koala. No more dancing for me. I'd love to tell you all about that night, but apart from heading back to Dave's with about ten other people for an after party and some shenanigans that involved shaving cream, a disposable camera and a blow-up doll, I can't really remember much. I passed out in Dave's bed next to Cian, a barmaid from the local pub who basically lived with Dave and Al when she wasn't working, while Katy fell asleep in an armchair and I'm pretty sure Dave graciously took the kitchen floor.

The next day Katy and I woke around noon and headed off to our first shift at the Walkabout. I was dressed in a cop's outfit, complete with handcuffs and a baton. I think I was subconsciously arming myself for battle – I must admit, I was a bit nervous. Katy obviously knew what she was in for, but for me working behind that bar took some getting used to.

It was pretty busy, even in the early afternoon, and I had no idea where anything was. I was glad Katy was with me, because she was completely outrageous and made up for any shyness I might have felt while I was serving beer half naked. Although, it turns out I'm a natural at skimpy work. Being the centre of attention is not something I have ever had a problem with.

Working as a skimpy is a different ball game to being a regular barmaid. We would dress up in little outfits – you know, the type you can buy from a sex shop (a cop's uniform, a schoolgirl's uniform, and my favourite, a French maid's uniform that would be guaranteed to land you a pay rise if you really were a maid) – and work behind the bar from about 4 p.m. to 11 p.m. serving drinks and chatting to the blokes. Usually they just asked us a heap of questions about ourselves (who doesn't like talking about themselves? I was starting to realise this was my dream job!). But occasionally we got sleazebags who would hit on us, while one memorable customer, a seventy-something-year-old man, spent hours telling us how sexy his nineteen-year-old Asian wife was and how he'd much prefer to look at her, blah blah. He even brought out pictures to prove it. I felt so sorry for the poor girl. The man was no Sean Connery, that's for sure.

We might have had to deal with the odd dickhead but we didn't have to clean or stock fridges, which was great because in those outfits you'd freeze your arse off. Every two hours or so one of us skimpies would grab a jug or hat or whatever we could find behind the bar and take it around the pub, encouraging blokes to throw in money on the promise of the top half of our clothing being removed. Usually we'd get at least $100 in our 'titty kitty' at a time, averaging us about $200 each in tips a night. Which sounds great, I know, but a few years beforehand the pub used to be standing room only, it was that packed, and it was more like $500 each in tips a night. The mine had laid off a lot of workers since then, so the town had gone a bit quiet and the girls were making less than half of what they used to. That said, neither of us were very good hustlers. We kept getting too caught up gasbagging with each other or the blokes to be bothered milking the men in the bar dry.

I had never been to a mining town in the middle of Aboriginal land, and the laws around alcohol sales are different there. To buy takeaway alcohol you're required to obtain a permit, and the licensing officers were constantly in the pub to check up on problem drinkers and make sure we complied with the terms of our RSA certificates. Many Aboriginal people in Arnhem Land don't speak English, or if they do they have very heavy accents. At first I misunderstood lots of orders and had to throw out drinks left, right and centre. But after a week I had the hang of things and could even speak a few words of the Yolngu language – hello, good, no good, cigarette/smoke and alcohol. And, just a heads-up, if someone asks you for a green can, they want a VB.

Some people go to Gove for work and never leave. Like my old mate Wilson, who works for the mine and has lived in Gove for the last thirty or so years. Born in the Middle East, he came up from Sydney to work for a while and never went home. I met him while I was working behind the bar. He drank rum and gambled, and if he had a shit night he would turn to me and say, in his thick accent, 'Ah, fuck this, I'm going home to get fucking stoned.' I thought he was a funny old bloke and on a few occasions I'd go over to his house for a drink. He'd make me sit there and watch Rodney Rude DVDs while we smoked Purple Haze (one of the strains of the controversial 'legal weed' that was flooding mining towns all over Australia at the time. I wouldn't touch the stuff with a ten-foot pole now but this was before I knew it could kill you). Anyway, Wilson found Rodney Rude fucking hilarious. I don't mind the bloke myself but watching Wilson's reaction to his jokes was *waaay* more entertaining than actually watching the comedian himself. He would nearly fall off his lounge laughing, 'Oh my god, that man, he so fuckin' funny!' Then he'd rewind it and make me watch the funny bit again.

There are also some people who come to Gove and never leave because they can't. While I was working at the Walkabout I met a couple of guys who were running from one thing or another. The local cops came into the pub looking for one of them because his family had reported him missing. Another guy had some interstate heavies chasing him because of a drug deal gone wrong. Arnhem Land is a very easy place in which to disappear if you want to. The fact that I didn't even know it existed until this point gives you a good indication of how few white people from the southern states would know the area well. In fact, the entire Northern Territory is known as a destination for criminals on the run, along with man-eating crocodiles and scorching hot weather. Despite these factors, or maybe because of them, I decided I had to come back as soon as I could and explore the 'final frontier' of Australia. The relaxed attitude, the way everyone seemed to be your mate, the red dirt, the four-wheel drives that lined the main street – the Northern Territory was the antidote to the plastic world I'd been living in on the Gold Coast.

A few guys at the pub offered to take us out on their boats, or take us for a drive around and show us the sights. I'd always say no, and I had a good excuse: I didn't get a day off. And as far as I could see, the 'sights' involved trees, mud, and water you couldn't swim in. I had no interest in fishing. Mainly, though, I just stuck with Dave and his crew, because being in the middle of nowhere I didn't really want to go and hang out with strange blokes. When I worked at the agency I used to get scared sending girls on boat cruises. What if something happens, I'd worry, and they get thrown overboard? It didn't happen, though, because usually in those situations the majority of the party was quite good and if there were one or two douchebags the others would sort them, so the girls were safe.

At the end of our two weeks, Katy and I spent our last day and night with Dave and Al, who took us for a drive out to the Rainbow Cliffs, where legend has it the spirits that live there keep the cyclones away. Later that night, Dave showed me a photo he'd taken of the cliffs on a previous trip – there were shadowy figures in front of the cliffs that he swore weren't there when he took the picture.

After we explored the cliffs and nearby beaches, we went back to their accommodation, a two-bedroom brick house with blue walls and permanent airconditioning. Dave cooked us up a huge feed of seafood, and Katy and I lay on the lounges, stuffing our faces and listening to Dave and Al banter on about the crazy shit they got up to when they weren't working. One particular story that involved LSD, a croc-infested river, a leaky boat and a shotgun had me laughing so hard I fell off the couch. The way they told it, they'd gone fishing but decided to keep it interesting by dropping some acid before heading out. Unfortunately, this was the day the boat chose to leak and they ended up driving it around in circles, frantically scooping out water as it struggled to stay afloat, and wondering why the water was purple (by this time the LSD had kicked in). Other Gove locals out on the water that day wouldn't go anywhere near them, which was understandable considering that they would have looked like a right pair of nut jobs. Especially once they got the boat sorted and then decided the hell with fishing, they'd turn it into a shooting trip instead. Despite the dangers, I knew I wanted to spend more time with these blokes – if anyone was going to show me a good time in the bush, it was them.

The following day we flew back to the Gold Coast, where I spent the next couple of months doing the Gold Coast/ Brisbane pub scene and private bucks' parties on the weekend. I'd stopped working in the agency's office altogether and skimpy work was my main gig. I was raking in the cash, with most two-hour pub shifts resulting in $150 in tips.

Being out on the road driving between jobs gave me a new appreciation for what the girls put up with. I felt bad for all the times I'd lost my shit with them if they were late. I didn't realise just how fucked up the traffic is in Brisbane.

I have no idea who designed the roads in that city but I'm sure they were high at the time.

I ended up losing an exhaust while trying to park as close as I could to the Down Under Bar, a backpackers' pub where I had a two-hour shift over lunchtime. Panicking because I was late, I reversed into a concrete loading dock, and when I went forward again, my exhaust was trailing behind me along the road. Ignoring the stares of pedestrians, I parked my car and did my shift, ever the professional. Afterwards, I managed to convince a passer-by to help me tie my exhaust to the rest of my car with cables from my stereo. I made it all the way across the city to Redbank, where I had another pub shift. I rang the RACQ, who met me at the pub, where by that stage I was selling raffle tickets in a G-string. Might have been a shit day at work for me, but it was a good day for the RACQ guy.

I'd started to plan my escape to the Territory and made a final break with my on/off boyfriend. I'd been threatening to do it for so long I think he thought I was kidding. I couldn't change who he was or what he wanted from life, and trying to do so would be soul-destroying. I figured I had to start following my own dreams. To my surprise he was slightly upset and made a half-hearted attempt to talk me out of it. Quite frankly, I think *he* was too out of it to realise where the fuck I was, or that I had gone to the Territory for two weeks, returned and was leaving again, to travel Australia. I had the perfect chance to do this now that I was working as a skimpy. As well as my Gold Coast boss, I had other contacts in the industry and the opportunity to cash in was huge. There were mining towns all over Australia looking for girls to serve beer in their underwear and I was planning to make hay while the sun was still shining!

So in February 2011 I flew back to Gove to do another two-week stint at the Walkabout and hopefully catch up with Dave, Al and all my other new friends. And that's how I came to be back in the Animal Bar, as the Walkabout's front bar is called, trying to stop my thick-skulled new miner buddy from being kicked out after he'd basically bullied the entire bar into putting money in my hat.

'C'mon, Wayne, he's not causing much trouble, do you have to kick him out?' I asked the bouncer, a huge Islander who wasn't looking too happy with Mr Muscle Head.

'He just threatened to beat up those two guys if they didn't tip you. How much have you served him today?'

'Not much, he's fine, tru–' I was cut off when my new friend barged over to Wayne and started poking him in the chest.

'What, you wanna go, do ya, mate?' Muscle Head asked him. He rolled his head around and began unbuttoning his shirt. Here I was trying to stop him getting kicked out and he was carrying on like an extra from *Road House*.

I looked at Wayne. 'Okay, maybe he has had too much to drink.'

Another bouncer showed up and my mate was tossed outside. Wayne came back in and started lecturing me on getting the blokes too drunk.

'But Wayne, it's not my fault,' I whinged. 'These blokes are so tight sometimes it's the only way you can make money!'

Most of our customers thought we were paid $60 per hour, because a few years back this had been the case. The girls didn't do jug runs then, they just worked topless the whole time and were paid a higher rate because of that. The locals didn't realise that we got a pay cut when the rules changed, so they resented having to put money in the skimpy tip jug. They never believed us when we told them the truth: that we were paid $25 per hour and had to pay half of our airfare to get to Gove. So we relied on tips to make it worth our while. And if that meant getting a few blokes blind rotten drunk in the process, then that was a risk I was willing to take!

CHAPTER 5

REALLY GONE
TO GOVE

WHEN I WASN'T WORKING AT THE LOCAL pub in Gove, I was spending most of my time with Dave, the big curly-haired bloke from the bush who'd shown me such a good time on my first visit. As a grader driver, Dave's work involved fixing all the roads in and around the communities in East Arnhem Land. His hobbies included speedboats, quad bikes, hunting and fishing. I was seriously impressed by Dave's blokey charm. Even though I find fishing as boring as batshit, and can't watch while men kill stuff, it was a breath of fresh air for me to meet a bloke who actually acted like, well, a bloke. I'm not saying men shouldn't take care of themselves but it's a bit depressing when you have to fight your boyfriend for the bathroom mirror.

I was supposed to be staying in a room at the back of the Walkabout Tavern, but I started heading over to Dave's after my shift ended around 11 p.m. He would always have something yummy cooked for me, which was great because the pub food tasted like shit. They fed us leftovers and saved the good stuff for paying guests. After a few days of living off cold bits of meat and watery vegies, I thought Dave's food was five-star. They say the way to a man's heart is through his stomach, but it was while I was eating Dave's meals out on the balcony, drinking wine and swapping stories with him that I realised I didn't want to be anywhere else. Dave and I had pretended we were just mates but after we kissed on the balcony after another night of great food, wine and company, we knew it was a bit more than that. Agreeing that we were having too much fun to be apart, we decided to just jump in the deep end, without knowing whether it would work or where we were going to end up.

I flew back to the Gold Coast and packed up all my stuff — that included retrieving my dog Chaos from his holiday at the boarding kennels. Despite the airconditioning, television and spa baths there, Chaos didn't bat an eyelid when he was boxed up and put on a plane. For the foreseeable future, the Territory was now our home.

Dave picked us up from the airport when we arrived after a very long day. We'd been travelling for about thirteen hours and changed planes three times. Poor Chaos. When I saw Dave waiting at the gate, I couldn't believe how nervous he looked. I ran up to him and gave him a huge hug.

'You really came back!' He sounded amazed.

'Of course I did. I said I would, didn't I?' I gave him a big kiss. 'Did you make me a roast like you promised?' I had been looking forward to his cooking as much as I'd looked forward to seeing him.

'Yes, Kel, I did a roast lamb with gravy and vegies for ya.' He looked amused. He'd told me that he'd never seen anyone my size eat so much.

'Did you make sure you put sweet potatoes in there too?' They were the best part.

'Of course! Now, c'mon, let's grab your bags and find this dog of yours.' Dave had been looking forward to meeting Chaos. After all, I talked about him enough.

At the animal collection area I saw Chaos in a cage being carted off the plane. He was wagging his tail, a big grin on his face.

'Holy shit, he's so tiny!' Dave said. 'I thought he'd be a lot bigger than that.'

'He's a pit bull, not a bull mastiff, Dave,' I said, clipping a chain on Chaos's collar and giving him a hug.

'I know, you just don't see dogs that small around here, eh …' Dave was right. Most dogs living in the Northern Territory resemble large ponies.

I insisted Chaos ride inside the ute on the way home.

'Only this once,' Dave said. 'I'm gonna teach him to be a real dog soon, he'll love it.' Chaos had lived indoors all his life. He had his own couch and enjoyed riding shotgun in my car. Somehow I doubted he was going to enjoy being turned into a 'real dog'. Not wanting to burst Dave's bubble, though, I kept that info to myself. I'd already turned Chaos into a metrosexual and there was no coming back from that.

Dave had left the house he shared with Al when he stopped working for the company that owned it. This happens a lot in Gove, because most of the time people move there specifically for work and they're provided a house as part of their work contract. However, once that's over so is the accommodation arrangement, which can be a pain in the arse but it's the way it goes in such a transient industry.

Dave's new place was a two-bedroom unit that belonged to his mate Phil. It was on the top floor of a three-storey block. The units were designed for mine workers to live in with their families, instead of in a donga (a relocatable tin building) on the mine site. You were supposed to have children in order to live there, but Phil's daughter had recently returned to her home country of New Zealand so Dave and I filled the role of kids.

As well as Dave, Phil and myself, there was a cat, a bull mastiff–wolfhound cross (both Phil's) and Chaos living in this little shoe box. It was a pretty hectic household. How that cat is still alive, I have no idea. Chaos would have eaten it for brekkie had he had the chance. Although after a week he settled down. This was probably because the cat nearly took his eye out. Well, I think it did. All I know is one day I came home and he and the cat were sitting side by side on the balcony and Chaos couldn't open one of his eyes.

I'd known that once I moved to Gove to live with Dave, being a skimpy at the local pub was no longer an option. I had become a 'local'. The boys at the pub didn't want to see the same girl behind the bar week after week. That was the exact reason the skimpies were flown in from the Gold Coast – it gave the boys something to look forward to every second Monday when the new girls arrived. While I had fun catching up with all the girls I knew who were coming and going from the Gold Coast, I was not going to be working alongside them.

So I had to look elsewhere for a job, but after working as a skimpy for the last six months or so, I was reluctant to go back to working twice as hard for half the pay in a 'normal' job. Unless I could score a job at the mine, the only other work available involved deep fryers and frozen dim sims. Which is horrible enough, but combine that with 35-degree heat and the humidity that comes with the wet season and it's like working in the depths of hell. Until 3 p.m. it's around

200 per cent humidity. Then the sky opens and it buckets down with rain for about twenty minutes, leaving the ground steamy and the air muggy. The water brings the mozzies and now not only are you boiling hot, you're also wet with a mix of rain and sweat and covered in insect bites. The only thing anyone should be doing in the wet season is sitting inside next to the airconditioner.

After a week or two I even thought about flying out to Western Australia, because there's plenty of skimpy work over there, but the flights from Gove to Perth were ridiculously expensive and boarding Chaos would have cost me a fortune. I didn't know what to do.

I was stuck in limbo and stuck in the house. As much as I hated to admit it, I was homesick for the Gold Coast and my old job. For the first time in my adult life, I had been able to pay all my bills on time and buy myself pretty much whatever I wanted. Now, instead of earning more than a thousand bucks a week and living in the middle of one of Australia's most popular destinations, I was trapped in a cramped unit with no yard, a thousand kilometres from anything. Except red dust, floodwater and man-eating crocodiles.

Dave kept reassuring me that as soon as he could drive out of Gove we'd leave and find somewhere else to live and work, hopefully in Western Australia.

Gove is located on the west coast of the Gulf of Carpentaria and the town is approximately 1044 kilometres from Darwin if you go by road. We planned to drive to Darwin as soon as the Central Arnhem Highway – aka 'The Track' – dried up. At the time it was a boggy mess due to the wet season, which lasts from December to May or sometimes even June if it's a bad one. During the wet, you can't drive in or out unless you have an army truck, because the roads are flooded and the notorious Goyder River Crossing is impassable. And you don't even want to try, because apart from getting swept downstream, everyone in Gove knows there's a bloody big croc that lives at the crossing. They've been trying to trap him for years but the sly bugger is too smart for that. Normally they'd leave him alone but once he started trying to take on vehicles crossing the river it was decided he had to go. However, they're yet to capture him, which is why you don't want to get swept down that particular river.

Dave sympathised with me but it wasn't so bad for him. He got to piss off for two weeks at a time out bush, building and fixing roads and airstrips in remote communities, leaving me to entertain myself in one of Australia's most isolated towns. When he came back he'd try to drag me out in the boat to go fishing.

The first and only time I joined him and his mate Al out fishing at Melville Bay it was about 8 p.m. and pitch black. The boys took me out to the middle of the deep, dark water and we stopped and dropped the anchor. Dave, who mainly fishes with a handline, gave one to me. I went to throw it in.

'No, Kel, wait, let me show you how to do it properly ...'

'Fine, what am I doing wrong?' I didn't care. I was only out there because he insisted I go in the first place.

Dave put his line down and tried to show me how to throw the line in without getting it caught in everyone else's.

'Sweet. Can I have a go now?' I grabbed the line from him and threw it into the water. It became tangled up in Al's. 'Oops, sorry, Al,' I said. Al just shook his head and cut the tangled line, handing mine back.

'Kel, have another go, and this time throw it *away* from our lines,' Dave suggested.

I threw it in and this time it didn't get caught. I'd finally got it. I sat and watched while Dave and Al pulled up fish after fish. When I got a bite it turned out to be an old shoe. That was the only thing I caught. It was so boring. It wouldn't have been so bad if we'd driven the boat around and maybe gone croc spotting, but we sat in one spot until the boys caught their fill and then went back to land.

'I hate fishing,' I announced when we got back to shore.

'Kellie, don't say that, c'mon ...' Al actually looked sad, as if he couldn't believe anyone could hate his beloved sport.

'Sorry, but it sucks. I can't sit and stare at the water for three hours. It makes me want to jump out of the boat.'

'You're only pissed off because you didn't catch anything,' Dave laughed.

'Whatever, I'm not coming next time. I'd rather watch Phil spend three hours cleaning his chair with a toothbrush.'

They looked at me as if I was insane.

'I watched him do it yesterday. I think the man had waaay too much coffee.'

'I don't think it was coffee,' Dave muttered to Al. 'Suit yourself, Kel. But I love fishing so I hope you don't get too mad when I go out next.'

'That's okay. I love drinking, so same goes for you the next time I ask you to pick me up from the pub,' I answered back.

To say it wasn't a great start to the relationship would be an understatement, but Dave and I were crazy about each other and determined to make it work. So we started to plot our escape.

While we waited for The Track to dry out, Dave flew in and out of Gove to different bush communities to fix their roads, and I stayed in town, praying every day to the gods of good weather that the rain would stop. Gove is a beautiful place but it's a bloody long way from civilisation. About ten kilometres out of town is the Aboriginal community of Yirrkala, which has some of the most beautiful beaches in the area. With their crystal-clear water and pure white sand, they seem almost untouched compared with the east coast of Australia. Surrounding the town was hundreds of miles of bushland, with the next community around three hundred kilometres away and unreachable by road for almost six months of the year.

With Dave away so much and the Pacific Fair shopping centre nothing but a distant memory, I was going stir crazy. The recreational activities available in Gove were not quite the same as the ones I had to choose from on the Gold Coast. Definitely no pole-dancing classes being held around town, that's for sure. Unless you count the signpost Phil stuck in our lounge room as a makeshift stripper's pole. We used to hold our own little dance comps after we'd been at the pub all night, until Dave drank a bottle of rum and decided to have a go. Dave, as I mentioned before, is built like a brick shithouse and his taking a running leap Superman-style towards the pole was never going to end well. Because I'm not interested in golf or fishing there wasn't much left for me to do with my day, so I ended up reading every book I could get my hands on. I became an expert on crocodiles, Mötley Crüe and why *He's Just Not That Into You*.

There was some good entertainment flying into Gove in 2011, though. I saw Kevin Bloody Wilson's daughter do her own comedy show live at the Walkabout Tavern. Jenny Talia was bloody hilarious – she's even funnier than her old man. Dr Elephant, one of the Northern Territory's best bands, were also regulars to the town, playing at the Arnhem Club every month or two. Apparently the lead singer was on *The Biggest Loser* a few years back and he's as famous to the locals for being on the telly as he is for being in the band. The State of Origin rugby league games are also a huge night out in Gove. The beer garden of the Walkabout Tavern would be packed out with almost the entire town watching the game on the big screen. It was pretty funny to me to see people get so wound up over a footy game. Half the locals had never even left the Northern Territory! There was always a brawl at the end of the night between the New South Wales and Queensland supporters. I support Queensland but to be honest I couldn't really care less about the game – I just used to see it as a great excuse to drink beer. But in Gove, walking the dog is a great excuse to drink beer. It's so hot and laid back up there that drinking is almost classed as a sport in its own right.

Despite the binge drinking and humidity, I attempted to keep fit. Dave was an awesome cook but he didn't give a shit about the fat content. He and his mates would spend the day fishing and that night we'd have a massive feast of fried fish and prawns, with mud crab on the side, sometimes cooked in sweet chilli. So I'd take Chaos for a walk around the town — literally around the circumference of Gove. But before you start thinking I must have been super-fit, I have to point out that this was only about four kilometres. Some days I would go for a jog around the footy field before it got too hot, but given that I needed to get up at 5 a.m. to beat the heat, it didn't happen often.

Apart from trying to keep the fat at bay, another reason to walk everywhere was Dave's LandCruiser ute, which was about twenty years old and covered in rust, cobwebs and red dust. Dave left it for me to use while he was working out bush, but I had no idea how to operate a manual car. He tried to give me a couple of lessons but they ended with me telling him I didn't even want to learn how to drive it, I hated it, and why would anyone want to drive a car with gears when you can get automatic ones? My attempts to teach myself to use the gears properly were keeping the whole town entertained. Quickly deciding that changing gears was all too hard, I'd leave it in first gear and drive through town at five kilometres an hour, stalling every time I needed to stop. I have since changed my mind, and having finally mastered the art of using a manual gearbox I actually find them heaps of fun to drive now. But back then, every time I walked into the local pub someone would call out, 'Hey, Kel, saw ya bunny hoppin' past Woolies before – how long did it take you to get to the end of the road? An hour?' And then the rest of the regulars would piss themselves laughing while throwing in one or two smart-arse remarks of their own.

The day I couldn't turn the ute off was probably the most entertaining for them. Unlike every other car I'd ever driven, this piece of crap didn't just turn off when you stopped the car. That would be too easy. Dave had shown me how to turn it on and off 'properly'. The conversation had gone something like this:

'See this button here? When you want to start, you pump it a few times before you turn the ignition on ...'

'Right, pump button thingy so car starts, got it.'

'And make sure this thing here isn't pushed in or it won't start.' He pointed to a piece of wire under the steering wheel.

'Is this one of the first cars ever made or something?'

'Ha ha ha, ya bloody hilarious, Kel. Look, please just pay attention cos I won't be here to show you all the time and if you don't do these things you won't get the car started.'

'Okay, okay,' I said, thinking wistfully of my old Holden Commodore, which was an automatic and pretty much drove itself.

'Now, when you want to stop, you push the kill switch back in.' Dave pointed to the wire under the steering wheel again.

'Cool, got it.' Geez, cars bored the crap out of me. 'Is that all I need to know?'

'Yep. You have to have a go at it now, though.'

Oh, for fuck's sake. Seriously, how hard could it be? It was a few buttons!

I did what he'd said and got the car started okay. Then I went to turn it off.

'Remember, push the wire in first,' he told me.

I pushed it but it seemed stuck, so I pushed harder. It still wasn't going in.

'Kel, you're going to snap it if you're not careful. You gotta push down and then push it in.' Dave was doing his best to stay calm but he looked like he was about to lose his shit. I soon found out why.

'If you snap that, you're fucked, the car won't go, so for fuck's sake be gentle!'

This conversation must have been on my mind when I found myself in what can only be described as a bullshit situation smack bang in the middle of town, outside the pub. This was great for all the blokes standing around watching. I'd parked the ute on the side of the road and set about turning it off. And that day it didn't want to turn off, no matter how much I jiggled that wire thing. I didn't want to push too hard and break the bloody thing – Dave's words of warning were still ringing in my ears. After about ten minutes I'd worked up a sweat but was still no closer to turning the engine off. Frustrated and very pissed off, I left the ute where it was, engine running, and headed to the pub, hoping that a mate of mine who worked behind the bar was rostered on that day. Luckily he was and, having a LandCruiser himself, knew what I was going on about and managed to turn the engine off. I ended up doing my shopping and walking home, leaving the ute for Phil to pick up for me, because Dave was away working and there was no way I was driving that heap of junk again that day.

CHAPTER 6

FERAL DOGS AND CROC NESTS

AFTER THREE MONTHS I WAS SO BORED living in Gove that I decided to join Dave on one of his work trips out bush. We were heading to the remote indigenous community of Ramingining, which is located on the edge of the Arafura Swamp, 560 kilometres east of Darwin and 435 kilometres west of Gove. You can get to Ramo, as the locals call it, by road, but in the wet season the only way from Gove to Ramo is by plane.

Small planes scare the absolute shit out of me. Climbing into one was the first of many activities that I never thought I would take part in until I moved to the bush. I swore I'd never go up in one of those tiny little planes. I mean, come on, every time you watch the news one of those things has fallen out of the sky. And they always say the same thing: 'We don't know what happened, old Jim's been flying for twenty years ...' So telling me I have more chance of winning the lottery than being involved in a plane crash is bullshit. But I went up in the plane anyway, that's how bored I was.

It took about an hour and a half to fly from Gove to Ramingining and I actually enjoyed it. We had a great view of East Arnhem Land. Dave graciously let me have the front seat next to the pilot because he'd done this trip before. Dave pointed out communities and tried to explain where we were in relation to Gove. It was pretty exciting. Although I wasn't completely comfortable with the whole situation. (Did you know some of those planes have windows you can *open*? You can fall out of those bloody things!) I pulled my window shut and tried to concentrate on the view instead.

Looking down, I could see exactly how isolated by floodwater we were. It was flooded pretty much from one town to another, cutting entire communities off from civilisation for months at a time. Other than water everywhere, the rest of the landscape was dense bushland. Fuck getting lost out there. At one point the pilot let me have a go on the controls. I'm pretty sure it wasn't exactly allowed under OHS laws, but hey, if he was happy to let me fly the plane, I wasn't going to argue with him.

After the scenic plane trip we hit the ground at Ramo Airport. And when I say airport I use the term very loosely. It's more like a bus shelter you would see in a country town.

It was covered in paintings by the local school kids and had a painted sign saying 'Welcome to Ramingining'. The runway was a dirt strip that was maintained by Dave and his grader. It was the coolest airport I'd ever seen. The pilot dumped our bags on the runway next to the plane, said, 'Catchya, I'm outta here', then flew off again.

We sat down with our bags and waited for a ride into town. And we waited. Finally, when it got to the point where we thought no one knew we had landed, one of the local shire workers came to pick us up. He drove us the five kilometres or so into town and I can't say I saw much on the way. My first impression of Ramingining was that it was little more than a few dirt roads, bush and mud, with no beach in sight.

Our accommodation, which the shire council provided for out-of-town workers, had four rooms, a communal kitchen/lounge room, and a massive empty yard surrounded by a tall barbed-wire fence to keep the equipment in and the camp dogs out. The camp dogs were the main reason I had left Chaos with the vet back in Gove. These dogs aren't pets, they're basically a bunch of feral dogs that roam the town. They attack in large packs and probably have all sorts of diseases, because immunising animals isn't a priority in most remote bush communities. In spite of the fence, one of the friendlier dogs had decided to make the compound her home. I wasn't supposed to give her food, but the moment I saw her I knew I would. The poor bitch was nothing more than a bag of bones, with a large wound on the side of her guts that no one seemed to care about.

'It's the way it is out here,' Dave said sadly. 'There are too many of them to start feeling sorry for them. You can't fix them, they're too far gone.'

'But the poor thing must be in pain. Can't we do something for her?' I hate seeing animals suffering. I was nearly in tears looking at this dog.

'They're feral dogs, Kel, they're not pets … This dog will probably get put down next time the vet comes to town.'

Despite the fact that I couldn't save her life, I decided to try to make the remainder of it a bit nicer while I could. Even though it was frowned upon, I would chuck her my scraps and give her a bit of a pat. Basic care in my world, but more than anyone else had ever done for her.

Dave and I shared a room that contained two single beds and a little table we could dump all our crap on. We did have aircon, which was a bonus because it was boiling out there. And wet. With shitloads of mozzies. The heat didn't bother me too much, though – I was starting to acclimatise to the balmy NT weather. You could even say I was growing to love it.

After we chucked all of our gear in our room and had something to eat, Dave and I set off in one of the council LandCruisers (which was about a million times smoother than Dave's ancient ute back in Gove) and drove a few kilometres out of town to where he was supposed to be fixing the road. I grew up camping and horse riding in the bush but that landscape was nothing like where I was now. Ramingining was even more isolated than Gove.

There was a small town centre with a medical clinic, a school, an art centre, a Centrelink office, and a mini supermarket they call the ALPA store, which was run by the residents of Ramingining. The ALPA store was a huge eye-opener regarding just how expensive everything is out bush. It was ten bucks dearer than the rest of Australia for just about everything they stock – I paid $20 for a tin of Milo and that wasn't even the jumbo-size tin, just the regular size. Another time I thought I'd get us some steaks for dinner but decided just to buy one for Dave after I pulled out a 200-gram T-bone and saw that it was $17. And it was frozen!

As well as food you could buy many other random items in this shop, because it's the only shop in the whole community. So if you're after a TV or some new shoes, you can find these things on the back shelves of the store along with all sorts of other household goods. Because the road Dave was sent to fix was the road that led to the town barge landing, the shop was very bare at the time. The trucks couldn't get through to pick up the supplies from the barge, which meant the town was running low on everything, including fuel. While Dave was repairing the road, which now resembled a swamp, the council brought in a truck body that was strapped onto caterpillar tracks and they managed to unload the barge army-style with that. But because there had been such a shortage of supplies, every time they brought in a truckload of stuff from the barge it barely made the shelves before it was gone again. People were lining up at the ALPA store like teenagers queuing for One Direction tickets. It was insane.

Dave had the inside info on exactly what was coming into town on the truck and he'd call me up. 'Kel, they're bringing all the food in now. Grab a couple of boxes and just load those motherfuckers up before the locals get in there … Oh yeah, and if you have a spare fifty leftover, grab me a pack of smokes too, can ya?' Smokes were around $40 for a pack of twenty-five. No wonder it was the first thing anyone asked you for when you walked into town.

We made it out of town to the road that takes you to the barge landing, got out of the Cruiser and up on the back of the caterpillar truck, hitching a ride to the site of the roadworks with another local council worker who was in charge of the strange vehicle. Because the road was so bumpy, Dave made me sit on a toolbox and set up a little umbrella next to me so I had some shade. He was romantic in a bushman kind of way. When we finally made it to our location I realised we could be stuck out here for weeks. The road was like a shallow creek with big boggy holes. Dave had already been out there for about four weeks working to get it up to scratch, but you wouldn't know it because any progress he made kept getting washed away by the nonstop rain. They were using gravel, sandbags and even fallen trees to fill the road back in but it wasn't working.

To make things worse, the barge landing is apparently a really good fishing spot and the local fishing fanatics couldn't stop themselves from using the road to go fishing even after being asked not to. By the end of my time there I was angrier about this than any of the council workers. The way I saw it, the more the amateur anglers wrecked the road, the longer it would take Dave to fix it. This meant I would not be going back to Gove any time soon. And at that point Gove was starting to seem like a capital city.

That was my tour of Ramingining and Dave's work site. After we were finished being chauffeured around in the caterpillar we jumped back into the Cruiser and set off to meet another couple, Matt and Jenny. Matt was someone

Dave worked with occasionally. Matt and Jenny were in their fifties and had lived in Ramingining for about two and a half years. I don't know how they did it, but then they were the type of couple who enjoyed fishing and hunting and all that bush-type stuff. I ended up spending a fair bit of time with Jenny, and she said she kept her sanity by visiting her kids in Melbourne and hitting Fountain Gate. A woman after my own heart.

We met up with them and went fishing off the side of the road, where Dave said they had been catching barramundi the week before (he wasn't lying – he flew home with about twenty of them!). This day we caught absolutely nothing. I wasn't surprised that I finished up empty-handed, but Dave is a master fisherman and even he didn't get a bite.

My first impression of Ramo may not have been fantastic but over the next two weeks it did improve. There were some pretty funny moments and some pretty bloody scary ones too. Sometimes they were both things together. One day I decided to visit Jenny while Dave was out working. She lived on the opposite side of town but because Dave had the ute I decided to walk. This doesn't sound like a risky thing to do but in a town like this it's downright dangerous. Not because you might get robbed or abducted; that sort of thing doesn't really happen there (unless you count alien abductions). What you need to worry about are the camp dogs. Dave had told me to carry a big stick with me but I just ignored him. After hanging out with the camp dog at our compound, I wasn't too worried about them anymore. I was an idiot.

On this particular day I was set upon by four snarling camp dogs as I walked through the community. I had no idea what to do. Should I run, or would that make them chase me? Or should I stand my ground? In case it ever happens to you, I can tell you that option two didn't work and option one was pushing my luck. I made it into Jenny's yard by the skin of my teeth. When it was time to leave I was holding the biggest bloody stick I could find. And I wasn't afraid to use it.

On my way back to the accommodation site, some young Aboriginal kids yelled out to me from their front yard.

'Hello! Hello!' they cried, running up to the fence as I walked past. They were so cute, with their big smiles and long curly hair. Looking behind me to make sure I wasn't being stalked by wild dogs, I stopped at the fence to say g'day.

'We saw you running,' laughed one of the boys, who would have been about five years old.

'Oh yeah, do you mean this morning at the oval?' I replied. (I had been doing laps of the town footy oval in the mornings in an attempt to get fit while I detoxed off the booze during my time in Ramo.)

'No, we saw you get chased by dogs!' they said, laughing their little heads off. Great. I was being made fun of by a bunch of primary school kids. To be fair, these kids were fearless and the dogs were probably terrified of them. After seeing one of them climb a tree in the middle of a croc-infested swamp, I knew that a few mangy camp dogs wouldn't bother them.

Another close shave was the night I helped Dave take all his work gear to the barge landing to be picked up in the morning. It was about 8 p.m. and utterly dark. Dave had me driving a tip truck, which sounds complicated, but it was an automatic truck so it wasn't much different from driving a car. In fact, it was easier than driving the LandCruiser, because at that stage I only had an automatic licence and although Dave had been teaching me to drive a manual I was still in need of about ten years' practice.

So I was driving this truck up the road when I realised I had lost Dave somehow. He'd been following me, driving the loader which he had been using for all the earthworks required to fix the road. I had assumed he'd follow me all the way to the barge, but then I remembered he was only taking it halfway up the road, to park in a clearing ready to use again the next day. He would then hop in the Cruiser he had parked there and meet me at the barge. But I couldn't see his lights at all any more. I saw a four-wheel drive coming towards me so I jumped out of the truck and flagged it down.

The tiny two-door vehicle was packed with four women, five kids and one bloke. I felt kind of sorry for him being the only man surrounded by so much oestrogen. I said to them that if they saw a big bloke with curly hair, could they tell him I'd meet him at the barge. They said no worries, and I got back in my truck and kept driving towards the barge landing. They continued in the opposite direction, heading back to town.

When I got to the barge landing I parked the truck and kept the radio on, singing along to Blondie. Next thing I knew, headlights blinded me and a vehicle pulled up. Thinking it was Dave, I got out of the truck.

But it wasn't Dave; it was the car I had flagged down earlier. Everyone piled out and walked over to me.

'Either you come back to town with us or we stay here with you, but you're not staying here alone,' the bloke said.

'Why, is there a croc or something that lives here?' I was paranoid about being eaten alive.

'No. Ghosts will get you,' said one of the women.

Great. Not only did I have to worry about dog attacks and being eaten by reptiles, I now had something invisible trying to kill me. The man saw the look on my face, turned to the woman and said something in what I'm guessing was Djambarrpuyngu, the local language. Naturally I didn't understand a word. He then turned back to me and said, 'No, no, it's okay, we just don't want you to wait out here in the dark by yourself.'

Either way I thought it was good of them to come back for me. They waited with me for the next ten minutes, until we saw more lights coming up the road. This time it was Dave, finally arriving to pick me up. After thanking the locals, we both got into the Cruiser and followed behind their little car, back towards town. I asked Dave about the ghosts they had mentioned. He told me the locals say there are bad spirits there. I've never really experienced ghosts or spirits so I'm not sure what to believe, but I'm really grateful I wasn't there alone, just in case.

In the two weeks we spent out in Ramo, Dave got one day off. To make the most of it we joined Matt and Jenny on a day trip to a nearby abandoned cattle station. Because no one had been looking after the livestock they had all run wild, even the horses. As we drove along the dirt track up the hill to the station they were everywhere, and some were in such good condition it was a shame they were too wild to do anything with.

Another thing Dave and I noticed everywhere was magic mushrooms. Because of the amount of cow and horse shit lying around, the mushies were literally all over the place. Dave loved them. 'Quick, Kel, grab as many as you can while no one can see us,' he urged as the car ahead of us disappeared over a small hill.

I hung out of the side of the Cruiser, jumping out to pick the best ones as we drove past. I had no intention of eating them – my drug use stops at weed – but they had disappeared by the time we left. The problem with Dave is that he's so crazy normally that he could have eaten them and I would never have known.

When we got to the old buildings that made up the station kitchen and workers' accommodation, Jenny took us on a grand tour. She led us through the main house, which had a large commercial-style kitchen, designed to cook for a big crowd. There was a living room, then a long hallway with four bedrooms, still containing beds (they looked pretty suss, though; I'd probably bring my own sheets if I was staying the night). There was a large veranda that ran along the length of both the front and back of the house.

Behind the house were a couple of cabins meant for station workers, then a shed with slaughter yards and more accommodation. To be honest, it was pretty unimpressive at that stage. The place had been long abandoned and although it had potential it would take a lot of work to get it going again. This was one of the reasons we were there – Jenny was looking at doing up the place and turning it into a kind of hunting lodge. I didn't appreciate how lucky I was to be out there, because as I've said I have zero interest in that stuff, but apparently I was in a hunter's paradise. Dave kept telling me that most of his mates from Gove would give their right arm to get paid to work out there.

Next to the 'lodge' was a massive billabong, home to all kinds of wildlife, including the famous and delicious NT barramundi that I'd practically been living on since I'd moved up to Arnhem Land. In the middle was a small island brimming with wild cattle. That was where Matt and Dave spent most of the day, along with the Traditional Owner (TO) of the land, his young nephew and another bloke with a video camera. It wasn't clear why they were out there on that day with the camera but I think it was something to do with a local TV station. Before they left for Buffalo Island, as I nicknamed it, we all piled into a tiny little tinny and the TO gave us a tour of the billabong.

I soon discovered that the TO was a movie star. A few films had been made in the billabong, including *Ten Canoes*, which this bloke starred in along with well-known Aboriginal actor David Gulpilil. I had lived on the Gold Coast, home to Warner Bros. Movie World and the Village Roadshow studios, for nearly seven years. Didn't meet a movie star once. And yet here I was, in the middle of Arnhem Land, floating with one in a tiny boat on a croc-infested billabong.

The billabong itself was pretty spooky, aside from the fact that it was filled with man-eating reptiles. The water was black, due to the tannins from the leaves at the bottom, and there were trees everywhere blocking most of the sunlight, which added to the eeriness of the water. As if this wasn't scary enough, Mr Movie Star, who also moonlights as an egg collector – croc eggs, that is – decided he would show us one of his egg-hunting spots.

So we got to the croc nest and I was shitting myself because I was sitting next to the side of the tinny and there wasn't that much between me and the lily pads. Then he decided we weren't close enough and steered the boat INTO THE FUCKING NEST! By this stage I was sure I was about to see a giant dinosaur head come leaping out of the water and into the boat, and I'm pretty certain I wasn't the only one who was thinking that. Somehow we made it back to land without any major injury, which I believe was an absolute miracle.

After that adrenaline-producing experience I decided not to join the blokes on their little hunting expedition at Buffalo Island. Instead I stayed at the lodge with Jenny and her niece and smoked half a packet of cigarettes. I don't even smoke.

But since I couldn't have a beer, I had to make do with what I could get my hands on.

I spent the afternoon chain-smoking and listening to the story of nearly every birth in Jenny's family. She has six kids so it did fill in quite a bit of time, which was handy. With nothing to read and no phone or radio reception, I was grateful for any form of entertainment.

Dave and the rest of the blokes finally came back just before dark with a boatful of buffalo. Yes, just to be clear, they carted buffalo carcasses in the world's tiniest tinny across a croc-infested billabong. Cos that's how we roll in the Territory. YOLO and all that. There was so much meat that the TO and his mate ended up taking it back to town and giving it away in the community. There was no way we could have eaten the lot.

When we returned to town, Dave went back to work but I was still wandering around aimlessly, looking for things to do while he was busy. I did go out to the job site with him a few more times to 'help', but that type of work really isn't my thing so I tried to avoid him as much as possible during the day.

We were sharing our accommodation with another group of workers subcontracted to the shire, and one particularly hot afternoon I was hiding from Dave in the airconditioning when they came home from work earlier than usual.

'Hey, mate, it's fucking hot out there … fancy joining us for a swim?' one of the boys asked me as they grabbed some towels.

'Where can you swim around here? Aren't there crocs all over the place?' I'd gone through too much dangerous shit out here already to get eaten now.

'Nah, the water's crystal clear, you'll see anything coming a mile away.'

'Well, maybe I'll come and have a look …'

I got in their work ute with two other boys and one of their girlfriends, and we set off for the swimming hole they'd found. It turned out to be a drain that ran under the road and was flooded, turning it into a little creek and the surrounding land into a swamp. The water near the road looked okay, though, and after I'd watched the rest of the crew jump in, I joined them. After a while it got too boring for the boys just swimming around, so they decided to use the drain as a waterslide and took turns being swept through the concrete tube from one side of the road to the other – all the stuff they warn you not to do when you're learning to swim as a kid, but luckily the drain wasn't blocked so no one got stuck in there.

We stayed for about an hour, and when we got back to our accommodation, Dave was there. I told him about the swimming hole, and he was keen to check it out, so we got into his car.

'Kel, this is a swamp. I can't believe you guys swam here.'

'No, it's fine, look – that water there is really clear.'

Dave just gave me one of his looks that said 'Kellie, you have no fucking idea what you're talking about'.

'Really, it's fine, we should be able to see a croc if it comes along. We'll just watch in opposite directions.'

Against his better judgement, Dave agreed to get in the water with me and we sat in a little rock pool next to the road. The water was clear around us, making it harder for a croc to pounce, but we kept an eye out anyway.

'It's not so bad, is it?' I said as I climbed onto his lap.

'No ... Kel, what are you doing?'

'I just figured I've got less chance of being eaten by a croc if I sit here –'

'You might have less chance of being eaten by a croc, but if you keep wriggling your arse around like that you'll get attacked by something else,' he said with a wicked grin.

'Oh sorry, I'll stop ...'

'No, no, that's okay ...'

I won't bore you with the details, but that was the day I could cross 'having sex in a crocodile-infested swamp' off my bucket list.

After two and a half weeks of living rough (Dave laughs his arse off when I say that – he reckons I have no idea), we finally got the okay to fly back to Gove. I can't lie and say I was disappointed to leave.

I felt like I'd just been on *Survivor*. Two weeks felt like two months out there, but I did learn a lot. Like carry a bloody big stick everywhere you go when you're out bush. How to drive a dump truck. That it's not just wildlife you should be afraid of in the bush, you could also be attacked by ghosts. How to fly a plane (and that some planes have windows you can fall out of), and most importantly, just how close you can get to a saltwater crocodile's nest without getting your head ripped off. All the important stuff.

CHAPTER 7

GOVE TO DARWIN AND OUT AGAIN

'C'MON, GIRL, TODAY'S THE DAY,' I HEARD
Dave say through my hangover. We'd had a massive
one the night before and I had no idea what on earth he was
on about.

'The day for what? Go away, ugh, I feel like shit.' I groaned
and rolled over without opening my eyes. My head felt as if
Ozzy Osbourne had taken up residence inside it, my body
was so sore it felt like I'd gone ten rounds with Mike Tyson
and I was sure that if I moved an inch I would throw up.
If he thought I was going out on a boat he was out of his
bloody mind.

'We're driving out of here. C'mon, get your gear, I gotta
get the ute loaded up,' he said, gently shaking me awake.

'Oh my god, stop, pleeeeeaaase ... I'll be sick,' I said as
the rocking brought on a wave of nausea. Then I processed
what he had just told me. 'We're driving out today? Have you
even slept?' Dave had been partying alongside me the night

before and I couldn't remember if he went to bed before or after I did.

'Well, a bit, but then I had to fix a few things on the ute before we leave so I've been outside doing that, then I went into town and grabbed some supplies and now all we have to do is get your shit on the back.'

The man is a machine, I swear to god.

Dave had got a call from his mate who had just driven through the Goyder River after picking up a LandCruiser in Cairns and was now on his way to Gove. The Goyder River, the biggest obstacle between Gove and Darwin, was finally low enough to drive across. This meant we were no longer stuck in Gove.

Dave and I loaded up his ancient Cruiser with all the stuff I'd brought up from the Gold Coast, including my beloved Chaos, and set off down the track to Darwin. To get there we had to drive roughly six hundred kilometres of really shitty dirt road, otherwise known as the Central Arnhem Highway. The track had only just dried up (well, most of it) and the road was an absolute mess because no one had graded it yet. It was probably a bit early for us to drive through, but we were itching to get out. Dave belted along the red dirt at a hundred miles an hour, expertly steering the car around the hazardous bits. I held onto my seat with white knuckles and a green face, trying really hard not to throw up.

After a little while, the nausea subsided and Dave gave another one of his 'tour guide' speeches, telling me the names of different communities we passed through and people he had met out there. He'd made nearly every road and airstrip in East Arnhem Land, so he knew the area well. As we approached the Goyder River Crossing, he told me what had happened the last time he attempted to drive through.

'We'd had a cruisy day at work tidying up the camp, refuelling and checking the scope of works for the upcoming jobs; seeing as it was the wet season, work was starting to get limited. Remember Cian?'

'Yeah. How could I forget?' Cian was the crazy barmaid I'd partied with the first night I arrived in Gove – and then passed out next to at Dave's house. She was one of the boys. Unlike me, she genuinely loved fishing.

'Well, she had some time off from the pub so she came out for a run. After doing all the work that had to be done, I thought we might go have a look at the Goyder, knowing it was flooding and was only forty kilometres away. Cian hadn't been out there yet and was keen to see it.'

'Why?'

'It's one of the major river crossings between Darwin and Gove, Kel – it's named after George Goyder, the bloke who basically founded Darwin.'

'Oh, righto.' I still didn't understand why the hell anyone would add an extra hundred kilometres to a trip to look at a fucking river in the middle of nowhere, but then there isn't a great deal to do in Gove, as I'd discovered.

'Anyway, we got down there and I put the nose of the Cruiser in the water. It was running fast but not too deep. Remember, that fourteen-foot croc lives there. I've seen him heaps. I didn't think it was safe to cross, so I reversed out. Then bloody Cian wanted a photo up the river so I put the nose back in and she got some snaps. The front of the car suddenly shifted a couple of feet downriver, so I slammed it in reverse to get out of there – but I had to angle in between a couple of trees, which put me off-line to get out. I tried to shimmy it around but couldn't, so I drove back as far as I could. Because I had nothing in the back of the ute it was light as fuck and the river started pushing us further down.' He shook his head. 'Had the ute flat out trying to beat the river but it was no good. The car was facing upriver and we weren't making any headway. Cian asked if we were fucked and going to roll over. I said not yet, I was still fighting for the win. Then the car started slipping in deeper and began to lurch. I told her yep, we're fucked and we're going to go turtle, and to grab any of her shit off the dash that she wanted to keep and get ready to bail. She was shitting! As you would. Then it happened – the Cruiser started to rise up, about to flip. I told Cian to get out and get clear of the car so she wouldn't get pinned. Out she flew, with me still trying to hold it. At the last second I knew it wouldn't be staying upright. I switched the car off to stop it from sucking a gutful of water and blowing the motor up. I grabbed my pack of smokes and lighter and bailed out as the car rolled over on its side.'

At this point in the story my face was pale and my nausea had returned. Dave continued.

'I fought the river to the bank and dragged my arse out, ciggies soaked. Called out for Cian and she was on the other side of the river. The wrong side. She was laughing her head off. Mad, that bitch! So the only thing to do was swim over and drag her back to the Gove side.

'Then it was time to get to work. The car was pushed up on a thirty-degree angle next to the steep bank. I got out to it, holding on in the fast-flowing water, then I dove under and released the hook on the winch, which took a couple of goes. I pulled the winch out and connected it to some paperbark trees and winched it up. I managed to get the whole front of the car out of the river. Then the rear diff kept getting hooked up on the lip of the bank. It took me a couple of hours, jamming some big logs in between the bank and the car, but I got it out. Meanwhile Cian had passed out right on the bank. Fuck, I went off. Feet dangling in the water waiting for a croc to grab her while she slept! But being asleep she got the worst case of sunburn I've ever seen. Practically third-degree burns, I reckon.'

'So how did you guys get back to Gove?'

'Well, no cars were coming down to the river bank in the wet, so we walked up to the track and waited for someone to come past. The sat phone was wet along with the lighter and smokes.' He grinned at me. 'We ended up staying out there. I scraped the road clear of rocks for my bed and Cian turned around with the shits. "Trust you to take the comfy side of the bed, ya prick!" she whinged. Funny as fuck. During the night we heard some locals calling out from the other side of the river. I knew them, so another swim across for a ciggy run was on.'

'Are you insane? You swam across a river with a fourteen-foot croc for a couple of smokes?'

'It was a stressful day, Kel.' Dave winked at me. 'In the end all the car needed was new oil, motor, diff, gearbox, et cetera, and it could be driven back to Gove – with soggy seats, of course. But that dickhead I used to work for refused to send them.'

'Is that why you quit?'

'Pretty much.'

Although Dave had proven to be handy in a crisis, I didn't fancy being swept away in a river that was home to a giant crocodile. I'm not a religious woman but I was praying to god that Dave's story wouldn't repeat itself.

We parked at the crossing while Dave had a smoke and I went to the loo for the hundredth time. We had to let the ute cool off a bit before we could cross the river. It was fairly wide with large gumtrees hanging over the water, creating shadows and adding to the eeriness. After I did my business I let Chaos hop down off the back of the ute to do his. I wandered along the banks of the river with Chaos, letting him stop every now and again for a drink.

'Kel, what are you doing?' Dave said when he finally noticed us dawdling. 'Crocs love dogs! Get Chaos away from the bloody water!'

Oops.

I called Chaos and helped him up to the safety of the ute tray, then got back in the car to attempt the river crossing. Dave revved up the engine and plunged into the water.

The next thing I knew was an intense feeling of being pushed sideways. I screamed and held onto the dashboard, thinking every moment would be my last. The river was higher than I'd thought and the car was sliding sideways along the riverbed. The water was swirling up as high as the windows and my feet were soaked for some reason. I looked down.

'Um, Dave, there's a huge hole in the floor on my side of the ute – all the water's coming in.'

'She'll be right – just put your feet on the dash.'

'But what if the croc gets in the ute?'

'For fuck's sake, a fish couldn't get through that hole, Kel!' Dave shouted as he struggled with the nonexistent power steering, the ute still not fully under control.

Just before we got to the other side, Dave cried out, 'FUCK!' and I nearly shat myself, getting ready to leap out of the window and onto the roof in case we were about to go under. He pissed himself laughing as we finally hit the bank, and asked me if I wanted to turn around and do it again. Did I mention he's a comedian?

We continued along the red dirt road, passing through remote bush communities every couple of hundred kilometres. There were 'shops' in most of the communities, like the one I'd experienced in Ramingining, but being a Sunday they were all closed. The communities seemed like ghost towns as we drove through, not a soul to be seen. We stopped once for fuel and some out-of-date Fantales from an extremely isolated servo. While I was paying for everything, the lady looked out of the window and said, 'Aw, isn't that beautiful?'

I looked at her, wondering if she was nuts. There was nothing but dirt, a petrol bowser and Dave out the front of the servo. I followed her gaze out the window and there was Dave giving Chaos a drink out of his big bushman's hat. As much as he pretended he hadn't, Dave had developed a bit of a soft spot for Chaos. Although I was worried about Chaos's health after drinking out of that thing – Dave'd had that hat for fifteen years and it looked like an ancient artefact dug up by archaeologists.

We were about eight hours into the trip and it was getting dark when the ute started to slow down. Dave pumped the accelerator but it just kept getting slower and slower.

'Shit, we're losing power in this bastard.' He pulled the ute over and jumped out, lifting the hood to see what was wrong. I hopped out too and peered into the motor as if I knew what the fuck was going on. After the noise of the ute blasting in my ears for eight hours, the bush was eerily silent and the air was very still. All I could see were the skinny, scrubby trees and tropical shrubs that are typical of the Territory. The air was warm and, being far from any city lights, the sky was full of stars. It was amazing. It was also a bit scary when I thought about where we were. In the middle of the Northern

Territory bush, which contains Australia's most hard-core wildlife – you name it, it wants to kill you.

'The fuel line's blocked,' Dave said as he pumped some little button connected to the rest of the shit that lives in car bonnets.

'Oh, right,' I replied intelligently.

So that was what we had to do every forty-five minutes for the rest of the trip. The car would run well, then it would start conking out, so Dave would pump the fuel-button thingummyjig and the car would magically work again.

After twelve hours we finally made it to the bitumen. I needed a chiropractor, I'd been thrown around the ute cab so much. We decided to stop at Katherine, fifty kilometres away from where the Central Arnhem Highway meets the Stuart Highway (or, as I call it, the turn-off to civilisation). Well, *I* decided to stop at Katherine. Dave was keen to get into Darwin and go out on the town. When he suggested this I nearly killed him. After that drive the last thing I wanted to do was go nightclubbing. Plus I hadn't seen a hair or nail salon for three months, couldn't fit into any of my clubbing gear since Dave had been feeding me up like a Christmas turkey, and besides all that I was falling asleep on my feet with suitcases piled on top of the bags under my eyes. So we found a motel room in Katherine, then hit the town for booze and junk food so we could mung out in front of crap TV while Chaos hid in the bathroom (we hadn't exactly told the motel manager he was with us, due to the motel's no-animal policy).

I almost needed sedating when I saw the Golden Arches. I hadn't seen a McDonald's 'restaurant' for three months and I was in heaven. I ate that Big Mac like I hadn't eaten for a week. Then I swore I wasn't eating any more junk food for six months. That lasted about six minutes until I discovered the minibar.

The next day we pushed on to Darwin, hitting the Hidden Valley Raceway to check out the V8s that were in town for the Darwin leg of the 2011 V8 Supercars. I really outdid myself that day. We sat up on top of the 'hairpin' hill on little camp chairs that made a bloke Dave's size look ridiculous – but then, being as big as he is, no one would actually point that out to him. Well, except me, but he never gave a shit what people thought anyway. This was why I liked him so much, I guess. Anyway, it was daytime and we started getting on the piss, as you do at these events. The problem I have is I can't really handle my piss very well, especially if I drink during the day under the sun, surrounded by the weirdest-looking people in Australia. It's a recipe for disaster. I mean, if you've ever been to a speedway event you'll know exactly what I'm talking about. I'd never seen so many rednecks in one area. Dave argued that they weren't rednecks, they were 'city people'. He finds all 'city' people, as he calls them, to be complete weirdos, and coming into town after being out bush for months always freaks him out a bit. I tried to explain to him that Darwin was not actually a city, more a giant country town, but he insists that with its population of around 150,000 people, Darwin is the big smoke, and nothing can convince him otherwise.

Finally, after about four hours of me drinking VB in the hot Darwin sun and taking the piss out of my fellow race fans (and, in the process, acting like the biggest redneck of them all), the race was over. Dave practically carried me back to our accommodation – because I found getting up out of my chair and on my feet to be quite the challenge – fed me a pizza and left me to sleep it off while he went fishing.

The next day we took off to Kakadu National Park, which is located in West Arnhem Land, where we did all the touristy stuff you do there. Kakadu is one of Australia's iconic tourist destinations, so I was pretty bloody excited to check it out. Although once we drove for a while I was glad I had Dave to show me around instead of paying thousands for a tour package; I reckon those tour packages are daylight robbery. We did all the stuff you can do on a tour without spending more than a couple of hundred bucks. And that was mainly on booze. My advice to anyone going out to Kakadu: hire a LandCruiser and spend a night at one of the pubs on the outskirts of Kakadu, where the locals will tell you all you need to know about the attractions and how to get there. Then buy a map and you're all set to explore. Well, that's pretty much the way we went about it, except we had our own Cruiser.

We started our Kakadu adventure with the Adelaide River Jumping Crocodiles Cruise, which is one of the better tourist attractions near Darwin. You watch these four-metre-plus dinosaurs jumping completely out of the river to snatch meat dangling from a stick that one of the cruise guides holds over the side of the (large) boat. Further up the river you can see blokes in tinnies, fishing with rods, and I wondered if they were really stupid, or just plain suicidal.

We camped under the stars at night at different campgrounds, surrounded by mozzie coils. Dave lit them up every night as it got dark and arranged them in a circle around our tents, making us look like members of some weird religious cult. We could have stayed in the ritzy resorts they have scattered around Kakadu, but unless you're really wealthy or get a good tour package, it's way cheaper to rough it. And then you can spend all the money you save on booze! So by the end of the night you won't even realise you're sleeping on the ground – as long as you keep a few bottles of red handy, the dirt really feels like a bed in a five-star hotel.

Despite being hungover to the back teeth most days, we managed to do a lot of hiking, which I hoped would make up for my night-time boozing and my new addiction to Allen's Party Mix. We climbed big rocky hills to look at Aboriginal artwork and hiked into the Jim Jim Falls, a seasonal plunge waterfall only accessible in the dry season, and even then you need a four-wheel drive to get there. The falls are worth the walk but be prepared for an obstacle course. We were climbing over massive fallen trees and huge rocks to get to the waterfalls – but then, knowing us, we probably took the wrong path. I didn't notice anyone else walking that way, now I think about it. I was so relieved when we finally got to the waterfall, but the water was fucking freezing. Dave, the mad bastard, jumped in anyway and swam off with his underwater camera, taking lots of photos of fish and rocks. Each to their own, I thought, rolling myself a joint and stretching out on a rock like a lizard in the sun while he froze his balls off. About forty-five minutes passed until he decided he'd better get out of the water before hypothermia set in. He took over my rock, and I took the camera off him and went to take some photos of the scenery when I spotted what I swear was a giant gorilla footprint.

'Look, Dave, there are yowies in Kakadu!' I showed him the photo then dragged him over to the 'footprint'. I had worked with a guy at the Walkabout pub who was a keen yowie hunter and had told me heaps of stories about them whenever I caught up with him for a beer.

'Yeah, righto, Kel,' Dave replied with an amused look on his face. 'I think you better ease up on the smoko.'

Working in East Arnhem Land in Aboriginal communities that are still very traditional when it comes to spiritual practices, Dave had seen some things that couldn't be explained – and that he wouldn't talk about, because even talking about that stuff can bring bad karma to you. For a man as rough and cynical as Dave to be wary of bad spirits, I reckon whatever he saw must have been pretty out there.

He wasn't convinced about the yowie phenomenon, though. He hasn't seen one in all his years of bush work, and he's worked in some pretty wild parts of the country. I still maintain that there's a big yowie running around Kakadu somewhere. My certainty is compounded by the fact that a 'Big Foot'-type creature was spotted walking along the Arnhem Highway one night a few years ago. Dave reckons whoever saw it was pissed and that it was probably just a really tall bloke wandering home after a night at the pub. Whatever the truth is, I had something to show my mate next time I was in Gove.

CHAPTER 8

KEL VS THE STUART HIGHWAY
- PART I -

IN LATE JULY 2011, I CALLED MY MUM FROM Darwin and told her I'd see her in a few days.

'Right, so where are you flying into?'

'I'm not flying down, Mum. I'm going to drive down with Chaos.'

'What? Why are you driving? Where are you going to stay? That's a long way to drive on your own. I think you should fly.'

Despite the fact that I was an adult and had flown the nest a decade earlier, Mum still worried about me – especially when it came to my driving skills.

'Mum, I'll be okay. It's just like when I used to drive down and see you from the Gold Coast except it's three times longer.'

'Fine.' Knowing there was no point trying to debate with me, she asked, 'What are you going to drive down in?'

'Dave's letting me take the troopy,' I replied. (Aka Troop Carrier – basically a LandCruiser designed to fit shitloads of people. Very popular out bush where seatbelts are viewed as optional and the average family has at least ten kids.)

'Oh my god, Kellie, you don't even have a manual licence!'

That was true. But I'd been practising for a couple of months and figured I was getting the hang of changing gears.

After our little holiday in Kakadu was over, Dave was due to head back to the bush, this time flying over to Milingimbi Island for at least a month to sort their roads out. There was no bloody way I was going with him. I can handle the bush for about two weeks at the absolute most, then I start going mad. The bush community shops don't even stock the *NT News*, let alone a copy of *New Idea*. I don't know how anyone survives in those conditions!

So for the month Dave was going to work out bush, I decided to head down to stay at Mum and Brendon's property in Burrumbuttock, half an hour's drive from Albury. We looked at flights for Chaos and me to fly down, but they were so expensive and when I got there I wouldn't have a car to get around the place. In the past, if I ever made the mistake of flying down to visit Mum, the first thing she would tell me when I got off the plane was not to expect her to run me around, she's not a bloody taxi, blah blah. I get her point: she works full time and has a million things to do herself. The only problem is that my mum lives in a town where the biggest thing about it is its name. Burrumbuttock has a general store/post office, which is not much better than the ALPA stores in terms of fresh stock – but I suppose at least you can buy a copy of *New Idea* (even if it is a week or two old). There is also a pub, though it's more like a scout hall with a bar in front of it. The locals are friendly but most of them are old farmers. Or sheep. I quickly learnt that in order to enjoy any time spent at my mother's house, I needed a vehicle of my own.

'Bugger it, I'm gonna drive,' I said to Dave.

'Kel, I haven't seen you get that car past second gear yet. How the hell do you plan to drive it across Australia?'

I convinced him I would be okay on my own. I was secretly excited about the idea of crossing the country. After the last few months I had well and truly been bitten by the travel bug, so I was more than ready for a new adventure.

After a few hours of driving around Darwin with Dave trying to teach me how to change gears properly, me swearing at him, the car and anyone in Darwin who happened to be on the road at the time, I finally mastered the gears enough to satisfy Dave.

We worked out a budget to get me down. Money was tight and fuel was going to be at least $1500, so there was no way I was going to be able to pay for accommodation as well.

I'd have to sleep in the back of the troopy. So we threw a swag in the back and that was to be my bedroom for the next few nights. (When I say swag, it's not the kind Justin Bieber uses to describe himself. In Australia, a swag is a heavy-duty canvas sleeping bag with an in-built mattress.)

The next day I filled up both tanks with diesel, chucked my suitcase in the back next to the swag, loaded Chaos into the front, kissed a worried-looking Dave goodbye and set off on my adventure.

I made it about fifty kilometres down the road before I realised I had no CD player. I had brought about two hundred CDs with me, so when the radio started to tune out I went to pop one in the car stereo. Then I realised it was the wrong shape. Shit. The troopy only had a tape player and I hadn't actually owned a tape since about 1998. So I drove along to the sound of the wind until I got to Katherine. I pulled over in the main street and searched a couple of different shops for tapes but couldn't find anything. Not even an old, obscure country and western tape from the op shop. I was destined to drive across Australia relying on my own singing for entertainment. Awesome.

Driving on, I made it all the way to the NT town of Mataranka, where I decided to stop for the night. Dave thought this was hilarious, because I'd only driven about four hundred kilometres. At this rate he figured it would take me a month to get down south. In my defence I hadn't left Darwin until after 11 a.m. and wasn't keen on driving through the outback at night, even with a big bullbar in front of me. Hitting a buffalo at 120 kilometres an hour can't be good for anyone's health.

I stayed at the Mataranka Homestead, an iconic NT landmark where the movie *We of the Never Never* was filmed. It is also famous for the incredible hot springs in the park. Not that I got to go swimming – I had to keep Chaos in a tiny section at the back of the park and he was most definitely *not* allowed near the swimming area. One guy working there warned me that he would shoot my dog if he escaped and chased any kangaroos. Since chasing kangaroos is Chaos's favourite pastime I thought I'd better stay at our little campsite and keep an eye on him. I'd parked the troopy in the 'dog-friendly' area and was going to sleep in the back, Chaos in the front seat with his lead attached to the door handle, just to be safe. That dog has been known to slip through the tiniest spaces and it was way too hot to leave all the windows up. Although the humidity of the wet season was receding, I hadn't left the Top End of the country yet and it was still hot as hell.

There was an old bloke camping next to me with his wife and grandchildren. We had a bit of a chat and he offered to watch Chaos while I went to buy some food and have a shower. Despite this I still tied Chaos to a tree. I couldn't be too careful.

After a hot shower, a hot dinner and a cold beer, I fell into a deep sleep, which is lucky because Chaos snores like a tractor.

I woke up the next morning about seven, keen to get back on the road. I packed everything into the back of the troopy, made sure Chaos hadn't gone roo hunting in the middle of the night, and helped the lazy bugger climb back into the front seat then went to start the engine. That's where I ran into a bit of trouble. I realised I didn't have my keys and had no idea where the hell they were, which is handy when you're about four hundred kilometres from a spare set. I kind of lost my shit and started to pull apart the troopy looking for them. Chaos stared at me, exasperated, wondering why the hell he was stuck in the car if it wasn't moving. The old guy from the camp next door came over to see what the fuss was about.

'Mate, I can't find my keys! I'm fucked – I have, like, 3500 kilometres to go and no bloody way to start my car!'

'Calm down, love. I can help ya get your car started – I'm an old bush mechanic from way back,' he reassured me. 'Now, what we'll do is just take that covering off the ignition and I'll teach ya how to hot-wire it. You'll be right to get to where you're going, no problem.'

His wife had come over by this time and was standing behind him, shaking her head and rolling her eyes. 'You can't pull her ignition apart,' she scolded him. She turned to me. 'Don't let him do it.'

'Why? What's the problem?' he argued.

'You don't know what you're doing, you silly old bugger!' she replied.

'Who are you calling a silly old bugger? I'll have you know ...'

I stopped listening and left them to it. I needed to find my keys – this guy's wife was right, there was no way I was hot-wiring my vehicle across the bloody continent. I'd have to find another way.

I ran around the park like a madwoman, checking the kiosk, toilets and restaurant, all with no luck. An elderly couple who were staying at the park told me that a mechanic was coming out to get their car, so maybe he could get some keys cut for me. Although this would cost me a bloody fortune I didn't have, I thanked them and sat with them. I asked them what was wrong with their car – it looked brand new, so why would they need a mechanic? The wife looked at her husband and said, 'Well, we wouldn't need a mechanic but someone put petrol in the tank.'

The old man looked down, embarrassed. 'Our car takes diesel.' And I thought *I* had problems.

Just after he said that, a man pulled up on a ride-on lawnmower and dangled a set of keys in front of me. 'These yours?'

'Oh my god, thank you!' I was so relieved. It turned out that when I'd bought ice the night before I'd left my keys on the bar.

I turned to the elderly couple, feeling bad because my problem had been so easily fixed and their holiday was pretty much ruined. 'Thanks heaps for your help, it looks like I'm okay after all … Um, I really hope your car gets fixed quickly.' Pathetic, I know. But what else could I say?

I went back over to the troopy where my old mate the bush mechanic was attempting to pull my ignition apart while his wife stood next to him, reminding him every two seconds that he was a bloody idiot.

'Hey, mate, thanks for the help, but I found my keys so it's all good!'

'No worries, I was nearly there. Just two more minutes and I would've had you started,' he said, looking proud of himself.

His wife rolled her eyes again. 'You just take care out there, darl, and keep an eye on your keys! Get a key ring or something,' she suggested.

'Good idea, thanks for that,' I said, feeling like a bit of

an idiot for not having one already. 'All right, I'd better get a move-on – thanks heaps for helping me out, anyway. Hope you enjoy the rest of your trip!' And with that, I got the hell out of there.

I hit the road again, taking two more days before I reached Alice Springs (it's about 1500 kilometres from Mataranka). I was driving at a snail's pace but I couldn't do much more than six hours a day on my own with no radio. The troopy was about twenty years old, and slow and steady was the name of her game. We'd get stuck behind road trains for hours because I couldn't get up the speed to pass them safely. I would have to wait until we had about ten kilometres of straight road ahead of us. The truckies were awesome, though – I had one of those CB radios, so I would get on the truckie channel and they'd tell me when I was okay to pass them. I had to be a bit careful with this because I was on my own. I did hear one truckie telling his mate about the blonde in the white troopy, and Dave told me later that every truckie on the Stuart Highway was probably looking out for me in one way or another.

I continued down the highway, stopping a couple more times before I crossed the Northern Territory/South Australia border. I passed through Port Augusta and left the highway, now headed for Mildura, where I planned to stay the night. Where the Stuart Highway was one long stretch of desert, when I headed east towards Mildura the landscape started to change and the trees became thicker, the ground greener. The air ten times colder. Luckily the troopy had heating. (Amazing, considering almost nothing else was working inside it.) The road took me through the Clare Valley, one of the most beautiful parts of the country. The town of Clare itself is set among rolling hills and vineyards and has old cobblestone pavements. All the buildings look at least a hundred years old. I loved the old farmhouses and cottages I saw as I drove past and fantasised about living there. Although in reality I couldn't bring myself to live somewhere so cold.

In Clare I had to stop to use the loo. Parking outside a tiny pub, I left Chaos on guard while I took care of business. Since I was at the pub, I thought I might as well buy some wine, so I went inside and looked around for someone to serve me. The pub was empty and there was no one behind the bar. Well, this is bullshit, I thought to myself. If they don't want to serve me I'll just go somewhere else. I stormed outside, all pissed off and self-righteous, when I noticed that the footpath was full of people and they were all staring at me.

'Is that your car?' asked one of the heads in the crowd as I looked past them and saw my troopy. It had rolled down the hill I had parked it on and smashed into the side of this bloke's old Nissan Patrol. Poor Chaos was still inside, looking out at everyone with a big grin on his face. Well, at least he was okay. It turned out that the handbrake in the old girl was on its way out and I had just found out the hard way. And since I was quite the novice when it came to driving a manual, I didn't realise that you should park the car and leave it in gear, not in neutral. Oopsie daisy. I swapped details with the guy who owned the Patrol, and kept going. Luckily for me he didn't want to involve the police because he wasn't supposed to be driving anyway. Something to do with the fact that he'd been at the pub all arvo and his face was glowing like a beacon.

After making quite an impression on the folks in Clare Valley, I made it to Mum's the next day without any more incidents. The day after I arrived in Burrumbuttock, the troopy decided to turn itself into a tripod when the rear axle popped out. That would have been a disaster had it happened in Tennant Creek or some other remote desert town.

As it was, the prospect of being stranded in Burrumbuttock, with only Mum to rely on for transport after all, was too much for me. Even though I love her to bits, we sometimes get on each other's last nerve. A lot of people think it's because we're so alike. I think it's because most of my adult life has been quite colourful and in her eyes a bit on the criminal side. I maintain that just because I went out with a couple of shady blokes doesn't make *me* a criminal. I don't think she's ever got over my becoming the local bikie gang's self-appointed mascot all those years ago. Then there was my ex on the Gold Coast who'd decided to throw away a perfectly good job to pursue his lifelong dream of becoming a gangster. Then there was the time I was brought home in the back of a paddy wagon because the friend I was with was driving an unregistered car. Or the time when I was fifteen and Mum had to take me to the other side of town to visit my boyfriend because he was on house arrest and not allowed to visit me. He'd also just got out of hospital after his friend ran him over with the car they'd just stolen, hence the house arrest (needless to say, that relationship didn't last long).

I'd say that hearing some of my stories probably freaks her out a tad. It's the way I tell 'em.

So I ended up taking over the lounge-room floor of my old mate Bianca's brother's place with Chaos for the next three weeks. I could have stayed at Bianca's but she'd just had her third baby and the only bottles I was interested in were red and contained 14.5 per cent alcohol. I still had dinner at Bianca's every night, but she'd be passed out on the couch with a kid on her boob by 8 p.m. The poor bugger would be up again by midnight for the baby's next feed. Back when we used to hang out, all-nighters included nightclubs and random hook-ups, but it seemed, for now, that wasn't going to happen.

Although I wasn't exactly stoked that the troopy was off the road, I was pretty damn proud that I'd managed to make it 3886.9 kilometres in four nights and five days, just me and my trusty sidekick, sleeping on the side of the road in the middle of the Aussie outback. Not many people I know are crazy enough to attempt that kind of journey – especially without a stereo.

CHAPTER 9

FRONT PAGE NEWS

AFTER I'D SPENT A MONTH LIVING ON MICK'S lounge-room floor, getting reacquainted with temperatures below zero degrees and spending close to $3000 to fix the troopy, Dave flew down from the Territory to drive me back up to Darwin. He had enough money together by now to get us there, and as much as I tried to convince him that I could sell the troopy and fly up with Chaos, he loved that old wreck too much to part with it yet. Still recovering from my epic five-day road trip, I wasn't keen to do it again on my own. Especially with no music and only Chaos to talk to.

Dave, being the type of man who doesn't need human contact to be happy, hadn't seen his folks in about four years. He always called them, but it was a rare occasion when he left his beloved Arnhem Land to venture down south to 'Antarctica', as he called the lower part of Australia. I'd never met them before and Dave was keen for them to meet me, so we decided to stop in and see them on the way back up north.

Although his parents were over sixty, they travelled more than most people I knew, taking three or four cruises a year all over the world, so it was lucky they were home at the time.

From Albury, Victor Harbor in South Australia was a nine-hour drive through country New South Wales and involved a ferry crossing on the Murray River near the South Australia/Victoria border (a much safer way of crossing a river than my previous experience). We arrived about 10 p.m. and Dave's parents were waiting up for us. I think they were worried we'd got lost. Despite the time of night, his mum sat me down in the lounge room with the family photo album, showing me photos of Dave when he was growing up. It was the first time I'd seen a picture of Dave without a beard; I was under the impression he'd been born with it. I also got along well with his dad, who reviewed books for a local radio station and had interviewed a couple of authors I loved, so I had a great time finding out about my favourite authors and what they were like in real life.

Victor Harbor was absolutely freezing in winter but still an amazingly breathtaking part of the country. We did a few 'scenic tours' so I could check the place out. It's right down the bottom of the country on the Southern Ocean, where Dave's grandfather was a prominent whale fisherman back when Greenpeace was unheard of. Fishing clearly ran in Dave's bloodlines and he used to spend his summer holidays out on the boat with his grandfather, learning the ropes. While we were driving over The Bluff (also known as Rosetta Head), he pointed out all his old fishing spots. I don't have to remind you how excited I get about fishing, but I was pretty stoked to spot a seal surfing the waves next to a person doing the same thing, closely followed by a shark fin. Okay, it could have been a shark fin, but admittedly this was back in the days when I used to get stoned a lot, so who knows what the hell I saw.

Dave's parents also took us for a cruise around the countryside and we ended up at the little island where the movie *Storm Boy* was filmed. That was one of my all-time favourite movies when I was a kid, so this was the highlight of my trip. But although I kept a lookout, I didn't see any pelicans. Mr Percival and his mates must have hit the big time and are probably living in a penthouse in Hollywood munching on caviar.

Another island just off Victor Harbor is Granite Island, apparently home to a colony of penguins, though I spotted none. I wasn't having a lot of luck in the whole bird-watching department.

After a few days in Victor Harbor we said goodbye to Dave's parents and continued up the highway. Dave managed to get us back to Darwin within two days, including a couple of hours 'sleeping' in Coober Pedy (well, we slept most of the time – as well as croc-infested waters I could now cross shagging on the side of the road in the middle of the desert off my ever-dwindling bucket list). I sat in the passenger seat and got on the turps most of the way back north, only taking a break from drinking to sleep. The way I saw it, I was doing my duty entertaining the driver with my awesome singing, which only gets better the more I drink. Needless to say, I didn't take in much scenery the second time around.

We made it to Darwin just in time for Dave to head back to work. He had rented a unit in Palmerston (a suburb on the outskirts of Darwin) for us to live in (well, mainly me – Dave was going to be working in Gove for two to three weeks at a time and would come back to Darwin on his week off) until we found a house to move into. There was no way we could store the copious amount of junk we owned between us in that tiny unit – the backyard was too small for a tinny, let alone Dave's big fishing boat as well. Then he had two old LandCruisers at the time, which we couldn't get rid of if we paid someone to take them. Both now had mechanical issues – the fuel pump kept cutting out in the ute and the troopy kept popping the rear axle every five minutes. I had found solutions to these 'little problems', though. With the ute I had to get up under the bonnet, blow some air through this fuel-line thingy, then pump a little rubber button about fifteen times to get the bastard going again. If I was lucky I'd make it a kilometre or two before having to go through the process all over again.

The troopy was easier, although probably more dangerous. Even after we'd paid three grand to fix the rear axle, it didn't stay put for long. Shortly after we got back to Darwin it popped out again. It was like a horse with a broken leg. Unfixable. But Dave refused to shoot it. I quickly learnt that when the axle popped out of the wheel I could still drive the car if I put it into four-wheel drive. Then I stuffed a cloth in the hole where the axle was supposed to be, wrapped it up in duct tape (my answer to many of life's problems) and Bob's your uncle, she was back on the road. To any other novice mechanics out there, I have to point out that this is *really* bad for your car so don't drive it around like that for three weeks at a time like I did.

With Dave back out bush it was time for me to start working again too, now I was in the 'big smoke'. Dave had been supporting my arse for the last couple of months, and it was time for me to get off it and earn my keep. Having realised when I was in Gove that working as a skimpy was my favourite way to make money, I hit up the local sex shop for some new work outfits.

I applied for a few skimpy jobs in local bars and ended up with regular shifts at the Airport Tavern, located just across from … yes, you guessed it, Darwin Airport.

The pub was a little TAB bar with a beer garden out the back. On the other side of the pub was a huge restaurant/ function area and some pokie machines, as well as another bar with a TAB up the end. When I first started working there I had no idea why they bothered putting a skimpy on. The blokes seemed more interested in the rugby and gambling than paying any attention to a topless barmaid. I could have worn my undies on my head and they wouldn't have noticed. This didn't last too long, though, and before I knew it I was 'in' with the regulars, who had seen so many girls come and go they were just waiting to see if I'd stick around. They couldn't give two shits about tits and arse; as long as you could pull a beer, do it quickly and have a chat while doing it, they were happy.

I tried a few shifts in other bars around Darwin but they never lasted long. One pub was owned by an ex-cop who still thought he was on duty, which, as you can imagine, does not go down too well in an old truckers' pub. It was a shame, because the pub was an awesome set-up for blokes, with a big shed out the back that featured strippers four days a week at lunchtime and after knock-off time. The place would be packed out and the atmosphere was great. Unfortunately the same couldn't be said for the atmosphere behind the bar, so I jumped ship after three weeks.

At another place where I worked, the boss used to save money on security by taking on the drunks herself, which was hilarious to watch. She was a four-foot-tall Asian lady with an evil temper and no fear. If you came into her bar and gave her any bullshit, you would be on your arse before you knew what had hit you. As entertaining as this was, I wasn't sure assaulting your customers was a great idea, and besides that, trying to get your pay out of the woman was like trying to get blood out of a stone.

After a while I realised I had it pretty good at the Airport Tavern and I made that my main gig. Despite one or two bitchy barmaids, most of the staff there were awesome. Going into work most days felt more like going to hang out with my mates. With Dave away working, and not knowing a soul in town, the pub was my main form of social interaction. I got to know many of the blokes who drank there quite well and spent half my shift chatting to them. I also became mates with the other 'toppies' I worked with behind the bar, and we would team up to do private jobs together, like golf days and bucks' parties.

In September 2011, a photographer from the *NT News* contacted me through the modelling website www.starnow.com, offering to do a shoot with me for their page-three 'Sunday Stunner' section. The page-three girl used to be huge in the '80s but these days not many publications bother any more. The *NT News* is one of the last ones that do it, and I thought why the hell not? I suppose some people might say these types of articles are degrading to women but I saw it as a work opportunity. I was new to Darwin; it was a great way to announce my arrival. In my line of work this kind of photo shoot is perfect.

I emailed him back and arranged a time to meet him at the studio in the *NT News* building. When I got there, however, I was greeted by a woman called Elise, who told me the other photographer had been called out to cover an urgent story and she would be doing the shoot instead. That was fine with me; I figured it would be less awkward working with a chick anyway. At this point I'd only ever done one 'professional' shoot, when I was living on the Gold Coast, and that was with my boss's ex, who is one of Australia's top glamour photographers. He shoots for *Penthouse, ZOO, FHM* and *Maxim*, just to name a few, and could make a sea monkey appear attractive. This shoot wasn't going to include hair and make-up, so I was a bit nervous. Especially as the *NT News* is the main newspaper in the Northern Territory. Imagine if I looked like shit? I'd have to move interstate. Again.

SKIMPY

We spent the next couple of hours in the studio, then up at the Botanic Gardens shooting different scenes and outfits. Elise was an easygoing chick and we joked around while we worked together to get a halfway decent shot. Finally, after another hour or so shooting in the gardens, trying to stay out of view of the local kinder group that had just turned up was proving to be a bit difficult. Considering that I was posing in skimpy lingerie, it was about time to call it a wrap and get dressed before one of the mums called the police or something. Elise and I had hit it off so we swapped our contact details before heading off in our separate directions. A journalist contacted me later that day and I gave him an interview that would appear alongside the picture that Sunday.

As you can imagine, the first thing I did on Sunday morning when I got up was go to the shop and buy the paper. I opened it up before I'd even got back into the driver's seat and there I was. A page-sized version of me in my favourite lingerie with the headline: 'It's Darwin or Bust!' I *so* did not say that! I didn't even know what the expression meant.

I rang Dave. 'Hey, have you seen the paper?'

'Yeah, girl, you look shit-hot, I'm proud of ya!' Dave was never the jealous type. Living in Gove for ten years, he was mates with heaps of skimpies who worked at the Walkabout and knew that it was great money.

'Yeah, but I sound like a dickhead – what the hell does "Darwin or Bust" mean?'

'It's an expression – it means it's Darwin or nothing.'

'But I didn't say that. I also didn't say most of what was written. I told them only to mention my skimpy work and not to make me sound like a stripper. I didn't mean literally write, "Kellie is not a stripper!"' (I have nothing against strippers, but I've never stripped in my life and I knew Mum would have a fit if she thought I had.)

Dave laughed. 'It's the media, Kel, what do you expect? Anyway, who cares, no one reads the article, they're just looking at the picture.'

Dave was right. No one gave me shit about the article, not even the boys at the pub. In fact, one of them cut it out and stuck it on the noticeboard in the bar.

So when Elise called me later on in the year to do another shoot, this time for *Signature Living*, the monthly magazine that is published alongside the *NT News*, I agreed. I had to model a heap of op shop clothes for an article about the perks of buying second-hand outfits. I was supposed to be there early in the morning but as usual I had a bit of car trouble, this time with the brakes. I'd found out they didn't work when I'd tried to stop at a red light, which was great timing. Bloody troopy. Dave, who was home that week from his job in the bush, got to work fixing them, but I still had no way of getting to the shoot, so Elise drove over to pick me up. I was running on Territory time that day and nowhere near ready, so she stood next to the troopy and chatted to Dave's legs (the rest of him was under the car somewhere) while I quickly got my shit together.

'C'mon, Kellie, I have to get this done by lunchtime!' she finally called out after waiting there for about ten minutes. I flew out of the door, hair everywhere, arms full of bags and a hairbrush in my mouth.

'I'm ready,' I told her, although she probably didn't understand me.

We got into the car and headed into Darwin city. 'Dave seems really cool,' she said.

'Yeah, he has his moments,' I replied distractedly as I started to slap some make-up on my face. It turned out that Elise had worked in Arnhem Land for a while and they'd crossed paths out there too.

'You guys should be in a shoot for an upcoming Valentine's Day special we're doing in *Signature Living* early next year,' she said. Now she had my attention. Dave doing a shoot for a magazine? I didn't know how I was going to talk him into this one.

'I'd do it for sure, but I dunno about Dave – maybe you could hide somewhere with a camera and take photos of us without him knowing or something,' I joked. 'Leave it with me and I'll let you know what he says.'

With my powers of persuasion and a bottle of Bundy Rum, I managed to talk Dave into appearing in the magazine with me. He really wasn't keen but he loved me enough to cop a bit of shit from his mates, which was pretty bloody good of him. Elise, Dave and I drove into a bush setting near our unit, bringing the troopy, which for once wasn't broken down. Dave wore his dirty old work shirt and shorts, and I wore a golden-coloured dress Elise had loaned me for the shoot that was apparently quite expensive. That put the pressure on, because the grass we were posing in was nearly as tall as I was, plus it was raining. Fantastic for my hair and make-up. Despite the rain, Dave and I, the professional models that we were, managed to ham it up for the camera, posing on, in and next to the troopy, as well as doing a couple of shots of him throwing me over his shoulder and carrying me off into the bush. This was pretty much the way our relationship started in the first place.

A couple of days later we were asked to meet with a reporter from the newspaper to give them a story to go with the photos. I was a lot more careful with my words this time. I didn't have to worry about Dave, though, because he is pretty blunt – he doesn't waffle on with total crap when he's nervous the way I seem to. The end result was an article that, again, wasn't quite what we said but close enough and not nearly as far off the mark as my page-three episode.

Because the shoot was done in December but the magazine wasn't out until February, I kind of forgot about it until I received a text from Elise: *Guess who's made the cover of the February 2012* Signature Living*?!*

Holy shit. Dave was going to kill me. I had told him it was a tiny little story and none of his mates would possibly see it. As it happened, one of the big mining bosses from Gove was in Darwin and got his hands on a copy before it was even released and took it back to Gove, meaning that half of Dave's mates saw it before we did. And they let him know about it at work too! Oops. I, on the other hand, was stoked and took the magazine around everywhere I went for the next week, showing anyone I vaguely knew.

CHAPTER 10

WAY OUT WEST

I COULDN'T CALL MYSELF A REAL SKIMPY UNTIL
I'd done my time in Kalgoorlie. Often referred to as the
'wild west', Kalgoorlie is an old mining town located in the
goldfields of Western Australia, a few hundred kilometres
inland from Perth. It has a reputation as a nonstop party town
because at any time of the night and day there are blokes
looking for a drink after work. The mining industry is 24/7
and, to accommodate this, so are most of the pubs in town.

My old boss from the Gold Coast had made me an offer
I couldn't refuse. A fortnight's work in Kalgoorlie in one
of the busiest pubs in the country at the busiest time of
year. In September they host the Kalgoorlie Cup and the
town is flooded with rich punters, racehorse owners and
mine workers more than happy to part with their money.
So I took a couple of weeks off from my job at Darwin's
Airport Tavern to cash in on the Kalgoorlie 'gold rush'.
The girls we sent over from the agency used to work two

weeks straight in their lingerie or bikinis and usually made a minimum of $6000 by the end. I was looking forward to collecting my share.

Looking back, the signs were there from the very start that my trip wasn't going to be a barrel of laughs. When I arrived at Kalgoorlie Airport at about 8.30 p.m., completely knackered after travelling all day, there was no one there to meet me. And every single person who had stepped off the plane was lining up for a taxi. I ended up sharing a cab with some random guy who for all I knew was a murderer, but it was better than standing in the airport car park for the next five hours in the freezing cold. Well, it was about twenty degrees, but coming from Darwin it might as well have been snowing.

I finally got to the pub, which I had dealt with for years on behalf of my old boss at the Gold Coast agency but had never actually seen for myself. I used to speak to the managers five times a week, but they had no idea it was the former office girl coming to town. The agency in town was trying to get rid of my boss's Gold Coast agency. I didn't want them to think I was there to cause any trouble so I didn't tell them I was Kel from the office; they just thought I was another blonde from over east. Maybe if I'd told them who I really was, Rhonda, the evil-tempered skimpy manager, might have spared me her welcome speech, which ended with: 'if you put a foot out of line I'll kill you'. Apparently that was her standard welcome speech and I was told afterwards not to take it personally. I didn't, because something I've learnt about this industry is that most of the women in charge are a special brand of crazy. I don't blame them. I only worked in the agency for a couple of years and that was nearly enough to send me to the nuthouse. I can't imagine what it would be like to deal with the bullshit that comes with running a stripping agency for twenty years. I'd need a permanent prescription for Valium and, quite possibly, a psychiatrist.

Anyway, I settled into my room, which I think must have been the old slaves' quarters because it sure as shit didn't look like any of the rooms they were booking out to guests. The toilet and shower were about two kilometres from my room. If you needed to go to the loo in the middle of the night and forgot to take your key with you, you weren't getting back into your room until the morning. But these were standard conditions for a mining town gig so I wasn't too bothered. What did my head in was being there on my own. When I'd gone to Gove, I had Katy as my partner in crime, and if the guys were dicks or the bar staff were horrible to us, we could go back to our room and bitch about them for the rest of the night. In Kalgoorlie, all I could do to debrief after a crap shift was call Dave. Which, to his credit, he handled really well, even at three o'clock in the morning.

I worked from 3 or 4 p.m. to two or three in the morning. The customers were great; I even had one guy, a nineteen-year-old engineer, tip me $400 in one night. He was on his own; after I first served him we had a chat and, impressed by my outstanding conversational skills (I'll admit right now it's a rare occasion that I'm lost for words), he decided he wanted to be served only by me. He wasn't sleazy at all; he was actually great company – and I think by that stage I felt as lonely as he looked.

Another pair of customers I wouldn't forget were the radio hosts from Perth who had talked their boss into sending them to cover the Kalgoorlie Cup. Their boss agreed on the condition that they were handcuffed to each other the entire time. Awkward enough, but throw in the fact that one host was male and the other female and you could see why by day two of the challenge they were at the bar ordering triple vodka, lime and sodas.

So the blokes in the pub could be great, but behind the bar the atmosphere wasn't so friendly. The other skimpies weren't the problem – it was Rhonda and her reign of terror that made working in that pub one of the worst experiences in my short skimpy career. Obviously this woman hadn't heard the phrase 'you catch more flies with honey' – or, if she had, she'd totally ignored it. I heard horror stories from girls who were stuck in Kalgoorlie, forced to keep working for her because she hadn't paid them for nine or ten weeks' worth of work and if they left they were scared they wouldn't get a cent. Her aggressive persona and constant threats made the place a pretty hostile environment. The fact that I was in a part of the country that I'd never visited before and didn't have a partner in crime to cheer me up when things were particularly horrible meant I was a miserable mess by the end of the first week. The only reason I didn't leave after that first week was that it would have caused major dramas for my Gold Coast boss and, besides that, I'd have had to forfeit my wages and pay her back for the flights. So I had to suck it up.

Because of my work hours I didn't get to experience the hectic Kalgoorlie nightlife, which was a shame as I might have enjoyed myself a hell of a lot more if I'd been pissed most of the time. The other skimpies were friendly but I never worked with the same girls behind the bar – they changed every night – so making 'friends' to hang with while I was there was proving to be difficult. Until I met Leah.

Leah wasn't a skimpy, she was a nineteen-year-old bar manager originally from country WA. And she was stacks of fun. On my second-last night I'd gone up to my room and was getting ready for bed when I heard music coming from the bar downstairs. I had Leah's number and sent her a text asking if she'd left the bar yet, to which she sent a reply: *Fuck no, come down and have a drink.*

So, dressed in my jim-jams and moccasins, I went downstairs into the public bar, where I found Leah and another barmaid, Lauren, sitting on top of the bar, each with a drink in her hand.

'What do ya want, Kel? I've closed the till but I'm writing down all our drinks, we'll just fix it up tomorrow.'

'Well, in that case where's the cab sav?'

She poured me a huge glass of red and then we sat around bitching about Rhonda and taking turns picking songs off the jukebox. Leah was obsessed with visiting Darwin so eventually we stopped slagging off our boss and started planning for her trip up north instead. At some stage someone pulled out what looked suspiciously like a joint and the next thing I knew I was in bed.

The following day I woke up to the sound of my mobile phone buzzing. Stupidly, I answered it, only to hear Rhonda screaming down the phone about licensing, stealing and written warnings. After a few minutes I realised she was talking about our little party last night and went into damage-control mode.

'Rhonda, it wasn't as bad as it sounds, we just had a couple of staffies ... We wrote down everything we drank, it's all good, we were gonna fix it up this morning anyway ...'

'All good? All fucking good? Do you know the cops rang me to ask WHY THE FUCK music was blaring from the Exchange at six o'clock this morning?'

Oh yeah, I'd forgotten about that.

'Just get your arse downstairs now, pay for your drinks and don't let me hear this shit again or you're on the first plane back to the Gold Coast!'

'Well, actually, I live in Darwin.'

'Whatever. Darwin, then. Is that understood?'

To be honest, that sounded great. If sending me home was supposed to be a threat it wasn't a very good one. A better punishment would have been making me stay another week working behind that bar. I was over it and never so glad to finish a trip away.

Meeting Leah was the one highlight of my stint in Kalgoorlie and, as promised, she came to visit me in Darwin a few months later, bringing along her favourite cousin, Kristy. They hit the town hard but I managed to kidnap them from Mitchell Street (Darwin's famous party strip, which had become Leah and Kristy's favourite destination) and take them out bush with Dave for a night. Well, technically it wasn't the bush. Wanting to impress my interstate visitors, I decided we were going to spend a night on a big houseboat, floating down the Mary River in the heart of Kakadu. I didn't realise that it's one of the most croc-infested waterways in the world. While Kakadu is full of wildlife, if all else failed I knew there were a few old pubs nearby in case we got bored with floating down the river.

When I told the girls where we were going, they asked me if we would see any crocodiles. 'I'm not sure. Maybe,' I said. 'I've never been there before but we're bound to see at least one if we're gonna be out there all day and night.'

That was an understatement. We saw three crocs before we even got on the boat. Then, as we floated downstream, there were crocs literally lined up on the shore. I started to get a bit paranoid and wouldn't go near the edge of the boat until I'd sunk a few beers. Leah and Kristy thought it was awesome. Much to Dave's delight (and my disgust) they loved fishing and spent most of the day trying to catch a fish. Leah ended up catching a lily pad and not much else. (I nearly died of a heart attack when she leant over the side of the boat to untangle it from her fishing line.) Meanwhile, I'd borrowed Kristy's copy of *Fifty Shades of Grey* and was trying really hard to like it. All it did was make me a bit frisky, but Dave, for once, refused to take part in any outdoor shenanigans because, after all, we were on a boat with two other people and I guess he wasn't as drunk as I was. Eventually I gave up trying to get laid and we went spotlighting for crocs instead. I was glad of the alcohol, because after seeing all those red eyes in the water surrounding us I don't think sleeping sober would have been an option. I'm not sure if it was the beer or the gentle rocking of the boat but I ended up sleeping like a log that night. Not even any nightmares about sinking houseboats and giant crocodile teeth.

The next day the girls still hadn't caught any fish, despite leaving the lines in the water overnight (considering the number of man-eating crocodiles that were swimming around in the water, the chances of anything being on the end of the fishing lines in the morning were pretty bloody slim), and I still thought *Fifty Shades of Grey* was overrated so we packed up the boat and went back to town.

CHAPTER 11

ON AIR

AFTER A COUPLE OF MONTHS WORKING AT the Airport Tavern I'd become mates with most of the blokes who drank there. One guy used to come in mainly on weekends, and although nine times out of ten he would end up absolutely shit-faced, he was never a problem when he was drunk. In fact, the more wasted he got, the more hilarious I found him. He thought I was pretty funny too, so when I found out he was in a management position at a local radio station, I told him he should put me on air. I was joking, of course. I had no idea what being on the radio involved and, to be honest, I didn't really think I could go on air without swearing. They'd have had to bleep me every two minutes.

Anyway, little did I know he took me seriously. One day, while he was still fairly sober, he offered me a job doing on-air promotions. I would have to get up at bullshit o'clock, drive into Darwin, pick up the 'Black Betty' freebie van, load it up with free stuff and drive to a landmark in or around

Darwin. The brekkie hosts would then call me and I'd go on air, telling the good people of Darwin where I was and what freebies I was handing out.

'Sounds good to me – where do I sign up?' I said.

Not so fast. First I had to meet with another manager. 'He's a bit of a sleaze,' my friend warned me, 'but ignore it and read through the script. If he likes you, he'll tell you what you need to do each morning.'

The next day I went into the station to meet the guy. Turns out he wasn't so much a sleaze as just completely devoid of a personality. And nooo sense of humour. Well, he sure didn't get mine. After reading the script to him I was positive he was going to tell me thanks but no thanks. He had interrupted me that many times to say I was reading it wrong (who would think talking could be so fucking hard?!), I couldn't see how he could possibly want to hire me. Obviously, though, he was desperate for staff, because he told me to come back on Monday for one week's trial – if I went okay, I would be the new radio station freebie girl. Woohoo!

I never thought I would be so bloody nervous talking on the phone. The first day I went live on air I couldn't eat beforehand and coffee was out of the question, even though it was before 7 a.m. I was wired enough from the nerves, and the butterflies in my stomach were the size of pterodactyls.

Somehow I made it through without swearing or clamming up, and the next day was a lot easier. By the end of the week I was wondering what the hell I had been so nervous about, and the station offered me a permanent job, so they must have been confident in me too.

Although the pay was crap compared to my airport gig, working as a skimpy wasn't something I could do forever and I didn't want to go back to office work. It was good to be learning something new, especially in an industry I'd always wanted to get involved in. So I kept my afternoon shifts at the Airport Tavern and worked weekday mornings at the radio station.

When Dave was home on a week off he loved driving me into Darwin city to pick up the radio station van. He would follow me in the troopy to my cross and try to convince me to give him free donuts and choccie milk before I went on air. I always made him wait until I'd done my cross, though, which he thought was completely unfair since he felt, being the boyfriend of a 'local celebrity', he was entitled to special treatment ...

I didn't serve my time at the station without my share of fuck-ups. One of the funniest incidents started smoothly enough – I had woken up early and had a hassle-free drive to the station. I got my van loaded up and, with so much time up my sleeve, drove to the furthest suburb from the station, Palmerston, which just happened to be where I lived. (This was usually a big hassle because of the timing – the drive into the city was about thirty minutes, but by the time I was loaded up and ready to head out to my destination, it was peak-hour traffic and could take up to fifty minutes to get there.) Arriving with fifteen minutes until my cross, I patted myself on the back for being so organised, and let myself have a little break and read the paper for a few minutes while I waited for the station to call me. When I saw I had seven minutes to go, I went to grab the station phone so I'd have it on me when it was time to go on air. That's when the shit started to go downhill. I couldn't find the phone anywhere in the van. It's okay, I thought to myself, I'll just call the station from my phone. Guess who left their phone at home?

'Fuck, fuck, fuck, fuckity FUCK' was pretty much all I could manage to say as I drove around Palmerston shopping precinct in a state of total panic, looking for a phone to call the station from. I found one, parked the van beside it, jumped out and called the station. Of course, I didn't have their number so I called up the Telstra directory to find it. The first number I got no one would pick up. The next number I called was some old dude's home phone, and finally, on the third call, the brekkie announcer from the station answered.

Thank fuck for that. I told him I had to do the cross from the payphone and he pissed himself laughing. He wanted to change my intro music from 'Black Betty' by Spiderbait to 'Payphone' by Maroon 5.

I think that sort of change would have been against my program manager's insane rules. He had issues about 'branding' within the station, as if we were a major-league footy team with a million-dollar sponsorship deal instead of a regional Aussie radio station. One day he pulled me into his office to give me a lecture about sticking to the script.

'You keep saying "99ROCK FM" on air; you can't say that, it's just 99ROCK. Please stick to the script,' he told me.

'Why is that such a big deal?' I asked. 'It's the name of the station.'

'Yes, but we're getting rid of the FM to make way for digital radio – it's a branding issue,' he said. No worries. He was the boss.

Branding didn't seem to be high on his list of priorities a week later, though. I was asked to come in on a Saturday, pick up the Black Betty van and drive it to the Darwin Showgrounds to do a special promotion on air for a whole heap of premium surf brands that were part of a huge sale there that day. But when I got to the station, the Black Betty van wasn't there. Another announcer working at the station called our boss who, as it turned out, had decided to take Black Betty home for the weekend to use himself. He told me to take the other van, which had another radio station's logo plastered all over it. So I ended up going on air telling everyone who was listening to 99ROCK (no FM) to come and see me at the showgrounds and pick up a $100 voucher for the sale. Problem was they couldn't find me, which wasn't surprising considering I was parked there in a van that had the FM bandwidth on it and nothing else.

One Monday I was struggling through my cross and just couldn't wait for it to end. I'd been quite sick for the last twenty-four hours and was trying to put it down to the fact that Dave and I had spent Saturday afternoon at Litchfield National Park, where I'd consumed my body weight in seafood. Something Dave had said to me that afternoon was ringing alarm bells, though. While I was lying on a rock working on my tan, he'd told me that he reckoned my boobs were huge compared with the way they'd looked the last time he'd been home. My boobs don't just grow for no reason – if they get bigger it's because I'm getting fatter. But I hadn't put on weight. This left me with one other explanation.

So Monday morning, on the way back from my cross to drop the van at the station, I stopped in at the chemist and bought a pregnancy test. I had no idea how it could be possible. Dave was working away for long periods at a time and when we did, ahem, get together, we were careful. Except for that one time shagging in a croc-infested swamp, which was a) a completely different type of risk and b) months ago. Anyway, I needed to rule out the possibility so I could put my mind at ease.

After peeing on the stick in a cramped stall in the women's toilets down the hall from the station manager's office, I discovered that I was indeed pregnant. Actually, I didn't realise this straightaway. I read the instructions wrong, so my first reaction was relief because I thought it was negative. Then I read the packet again and nearly fell on the floor. What the fuck was going on? I couldn't have a baby. I was too young. Then I remembered that I was twenty-nine, not nineteen. What was I going to do, wait another five years and practically be a grandma by the time my kid was ten? My own grandmother wasn't even fifty when I was born! But I was worried that Dave and I wouldn't be able to cope with a baby. Our relationship was a bit rocky at times, due to our different lifestyles and the little time we spent together.

I'd started to get homesick again for the east coast, to the point where I was seriously considering moving back over, even if I just returned to Queensland. Sometimes living in

Darwin feels like living in a foreign country. The fact that it's closer to Bali than any major Australian city just reinforces that feeling for me. In Darwin everyone kind of sticks together because it's so isolated from the east coast. This is why I'd loved Darwin in the first place, but after a while the feeling gets a little depressing, especially as life goes on for everyone else down south and you're missing out on all the birthdays, weddings, funerals and christenings. When you call your family you hear about all these events but you don't feel part of them. Coming from a family that has always valued celebrating these things together, it had been hard for me to miss out on everything that happened. For some reason, when I was on the Gold Coast I hadn't felt this way. Maybe it's because I was still on the same side of the country and still got east coast news and TV shows. Even the ads on Darwin television are different from those in the rest of the country ... well, except Cairns. You don't get ads on TV down south warning you about croc attacks and spruiking new windscreen wipers for the wet season.

That feeling as if I was living in limbo was starting to come over me again. I felt like I was just biding my time until Dave finally agreed to leave Gove. He'd been promising me for over twelve months that as soon as he found a good job in Darwin, he'd move over for good. This was nowhere near happening. As much as I wanted to be with him, what was the point if I only saw him a few days a month? Then there was the small problem of Chaos, the dog who thinks he's human. I'd have to figure out how to get him used to living outside like a real dog. He was going to hate it.

I called Dave later on that day, once I'd dealt with the shock myself. 'You're not going to believe this but I'm pregnant,' I told him.

'How the hell did that happen?'

'How do you think?' I wasn't in the mood for mucking around.

'I know, it's just that we've hardly been in the same town for the last couple of months. The odds of you getting knocked up were pretty slim! Oh well, I guess this explains why you look like you've been stuffing your bra with chicken fillets lately.'

Clearly Dave didn't find this situation as big a deal as I did. Here I was, pregnant and pretty much alone, four thousand kilometres from my mum and over a thousand kilometres from my boyfriend, who thought he was a fucking comedian.

'This is serious, Dave. What are we going to do? I can't have a baby the way things are at the moment. I'm struggling as it is with you being away. It wouldn't be so bad if I lived closer to my family.'

'Of course you can have it. It'll be cool! Especially if it has your looks and my amazing brains.' He thought that was pretty funny.

'What the hell does that mean? I'm not an idiot!'

'Settle down, Kel, I was joking. Look, I'll be home soon and we'll work it all out. I'll start asking around about work over in Darwin. By the time the baby is born, we should be settled.'

He sounded pretty happy about the situation. I wanted the baby as much as he did, but I was slightly more realistic about things. I was worried about being stuck in Darwin, so far from my family, alone for weeks at a time with a tiny baby. I had a few mates up there but I hadn't been there long enough to have a solid support network. It wasn't an ideal situation. We had about eight months to change it, though, and as they say, there is never a 'right' time to have a baby. So I pushed my doubts aside and finally allowed myself to feel excited.

CHAPTER 12

GRID GIRL

WHILE THE REST OF AUSTRALIA IS FREEZING its arse off in the middle of winter, relying on central heating and soup to get through the cold months, Darwin enjoys temperatures of around twenty-seven degrees during the day. When at night it drops to about eighteen degrees, the locals announce that it's 'freezing' and put on a long-sleeved shirt to beat the chill. This is tourist season, when southerners escape their winter and come up to enjoy the heat of the Top End without being washed out by rain every afternoon. The humidity eases over the dry season, making it bearable to go outside again. It's the time when Darwin's famous Mindil markets open, with the lights and stalls lining Mindil Beach almost making you feel like you're on holiday in Thailand. Locals cash in when they can, selling everything from cheap imported jewellery to traditional indigenous art. Another great day at Mindil Beach is the annual Beer Can Regatta, when locals build boats out of – you guessed it –

beer cans, and then race each other. It truly is a magnificent event and I think there should be more of them. I mean, first you get to drink the beer, then you get to build a boat from the empty cans, and then you get to race it against other local yahoos while drinking more beer. That's my kinda sport! And while we only ever attended the Beer Can Regatta as spectators, competing in it is something I'm keen to tick off my bucket list.

When we went to the Mindil markets, it felt like the whole of Darwin was there. It's a crowded, noisy mix of crafts and food stalls. There's almost every type of food you can think of – although once I was pregnant I couldn't stand to be around the smells of the different types of food cooking. It's not just any old market, either – it's more like a festival. Lanterns line the beach as the sun sets, and there's live music and a grassy area where you can lie around on a blanket drinking wine and soaking up the atmosphere (something else I couldn't really do once I was pregnant).

Halfway through the dry season, the V8 Supercars make their way back to Darwin. Somehow, before I found out that I had a baby on board, I had landed a gig as a Grid Girl for one of the V8 utes. My job entailed hanging around in the pit lane all day, talking to V8 fans in between holding a flag on the racetrack every couple of hours when the utes were racing. Probably one of the easiest jobs in the world, but I like to turn everything I do into a bit of a challenge.

My first hurdle involved a broken strap on the only pair of heels I had in Darwin. I was quite proud of myself for solving the problem with my old mate superglue. Until I forgot and rubbed my eyes before washing my hands. The stinging began immediately, and I shoved my head under a tap, ruining my make-up and wetting half my hair, which I had just straightened. But at that stage I couldn't give a fuck about my hair, I was too busy worrying about my eye and whether or not the bloody thing would ever open again. The glue didn't seal my eye shut, though. Instead, it balled up and I managed to get it out after about ten minutes of sticking my fingers in my eye. I probably don't have to tell you how red my eyes were after that, but just in case you can't picture it, let me say my eye was like a road map. Out came the eye drops. They kind of cleared my eyes but I still had to go easy on the eye make-up. Luckily I had to wear sunnies most of the day, anyway. Now well and truly running behind schedule, I fixed my hair and jumped in my car – a tiny two-door Suzuki Swift hatchback that Dave had bought me after the troopy popped an axle for the millionth time.

This brings me to challenge number two: getting to the Hidden Valley racetrack on time without blowing a tyre. Although Darwin is a capital city and Hidden Valley one of its major drawcards, the racetrack still looks like an open paddock, with dirt tracks and unsealed car parks. Which would have been okay if I was driving the troopy – but my little matchbox car wasn't really built to take on roads that had obviously been graded by a drunk monkey. The rocks sticking out of the track were like boulders. By the time I arrived, I was hideously late. The last thing I was worried about was my tyres as I flew through the gates to the racetrack and down the hill to meet the team I was working for.

I was greeted by a tough-talking Kiwi chick who had booked me for the day. She handed over my uniform and pushed me in the direction of the ladies toilets, telling me to hurry up and get changed. I did as I was told and emerged wearing a teeny yellow nylon minidress with a Bob Jane T-Marts logo on the front. I was working for his nephew, Kim Jane, who was racing one of the V8 utes.

Then it was time to do a photo shoot with the ute I was 'representing'. So there I was in the middle of a massive crowd, climbing on top of a V8 ute in the shortest dress I'd ever worn outside of a skimpy bar, acting like it was perfectly normal and I did this shit every day.

If you had told me a year earlier that I'd be working on the grid for the V8 utes I would have laughed my arse off.

Especially if you had told me I'd be pregnant as well. (I was only about eight or nine weeks along, so luckily I could get away with working for a little while longer.)

On the Gold Coast I had about as much chance of getting a position at the V8s as I would scoring a leading role opposite Chris Hemsworth in his next Hollywood blockbuster. But Darwin was a bit more laid back and there were a whole heap of local girls working in the pit lane that day. The Territory is home to some absolute stunners and I noticed that after that weekend a few of them really got into the modelling scene. Unlike the Gold Coast models I knew, whose style was mainly *ZOO* magazine with a strong focus on breast size, these girls were more catwalk-style models with natural boobs and long legs.

At 163 centimetres I felt like a midget standing next to half of them, even in my heels. If I had a bigger set of boobs (or $10,000 to buy a pair) I would definitely fall into the former modelling category. To do anything in fashion it's a well-known fact you need to be 170 centimetres minimum. But, hey, at twenty-nine I wasn't all that worried about furthering my career in modelling. I'm confident but not delusional. I was probably the only girl over twenty-five representing the V8s that day. Definitely the only one up the duff. And, just quietly, I was pretty bloody proud of that.

We Grid Girls were all expected to be on the grid with our respective teams' flags at the start of every race, and in between races we were to hang out in the pit lane, handing out promo gear and chatting to the V8 fans. While I was standing outside my team's promo tent, a familiar-looking bloke approached me for an interview, his mate in tow holding a video camera.

'I'll just introduce ya, and then you say whatever you want really – you could do a little spiel for your race team, you know, promote them a bit,' he suggested.

I was a bit nervous with the camera pointed at me, and when I'm nervous, instead of shutting the fuck up, I tend to ramble on with pointless bullshit.

Before he walked off afterwards I had to ask him, 'Mate, you look really familiar – where do I know you from? Do you drink at the Airport Tavern?'

Before he could say anything I read the tag on his shirt. 'Oh my god, you're Phil O'Brien! I love you! Holy shit, this is awesome, I love your work!'

Phil O'Brien is a Territory icon: a comedian, an author, and he has a couple of DVDs that rival Russell Coight's *All Aussie Adventures*. He's your typical Aussie larrikin and loves to take the piss out of himself. I'd been following his work for a while and thought he was pretty inspiring. I also thought he would make a great drinking buddy, because the man can spin a hell of a yarn.

'Oh, geez, um, thanks,' he said, looking at me as if I was a crazy person who might attack him.

We chatted for about ten minutes. By the time he walked off, I was pretty sure he'd changed his mind about my sanity because we'd swapped numbers and planned to meet up for a beer sometime. A beer with Phil O'Brien! I was on cloud nine. First I was working for a famous race car team, and now I had just met one of my idols!

Most of the other girls were friendly – one of them was an ex-stripper I used to work with on the Gold Coast, so it was great to catch up with her. She'd been travelling the whole of Australia with the race team she was working for. I was pretty envious of that gig – getting paid to go around the country with a bunch of famous race teams and attend all the after parties. If I hadn't been pregnant I would have begged her to take me along too.

While the majority of the girls were awesome, and half of them I'm now friends with, I did have a bit of a run-in with one who I'd worked with at a party a month or so earlier. When we'd first met at the job I'd complimented her on her dress, which although it was completely over the top for a shed party in rural Darwin – especially as she would be taking it off – was really nice. Her response was to tell me not to feel too intimidated by her 'as I'm a *ZOO* model, you know'. At first I thought she was joking, but after talking to her for another five minutes it became apparent that this eighteen-year-old blonde with a face like Sarah Jessica Parker's was serious. Then I found out that her biggest ambition in life was to do a spread for *Playboy*. It was only a year or so earlier I'd been sitting in the VIP section of the *Penthouse* Pet of the Year party in Brisbane, thanks to my boss sponsoring one of the girls and providing all of the entertainment that night, and now here I was sitting in some bloke's shed listening to the ramblings of a delusional teenager who seemed to think I was a complete idiot. I couldn't help but feel like there was something wrong with the whole situation.

A few days later I was talking to another Darwin-based girl who showed me the *ZOO* magazine article this girl had featured in. It was a section of the mag where girls can send in pics of themselves and *ZOO* would publish them. That is, anybody could send in a pic and it would probably be published.

So, even though I like to think I'm above the bitchiness that can go with an industry dominated by females, I must admit it gave me a bit of a giggle to see that Miss *ZOO* Model had a promo role at the V8s as well. Dressed in a green T-shirt, white knee-length shorts and white tennis shoes, she didn't look like a happy camper. I tried to say hello to her but all I got in reply was a filthy look. Not surprising given that the rest of us girls were decked out in micro-dresses and heels …

Before long it was time for one of the last races of the weekend. And my third and final challenge for the day. All us Grid Girls were called back to the racetrack and instructed to take our places with our flags. This particular race was being filmed live for Channel 7. I was the only one working for a team solo – all the other girls were working in pairs – because they'd only booked one girl to represent the ute. That was fine until I had to go on the track.

Because I was the only girl working by herself I was made to stand at the very front of the pack. Being up the very front, on my own, with a camera in my face was pretty daunting, even for a show pony like me. Plus I was holding a flag that was twice my height and probably around my own body weight. This is hard enough to do in decent weather, but the afternoon had brought with it huge gusts of wind.

While I was standing on the track holding the enormous flag, in front of live TV cameras and hundreds of spectators, one such gust of wind caught my flag, effectively turning it into a parachute and nearly blowing me off the track. The Kiwi woman ran over and grabbed the flag, telling me not to worry and just to stand with my hands on my hips looking straight ahead. At this point I wanted to be standing at the bar, downing shots of tequila, but I stood still, plastered a smile on my face and stared in front of me. After what felt like five hours (probably about a minute and a half) we were told to leave the track so the race could start.

I walked over to my team's truck, wondering how expensive it would be to move to Siberia, when the team leader came over to assure me that the flag incident wasn't my fault and not to stress about it. That was nice of her but she wasn't the one who nearly did a Mary Poppins impersonation live on national television. I got over my embarrassment when I decided that most of the people watching the race were probably drunk by that stage in the day and would never have noticed. And I keep telling myself that.

CHAPTER 13

BROOME OR BUST

I WAS TEN WEEKS PREGNANT AND FIGHTING 'morning' sickness for the better part of each day and night when I flew out to Broome for my final skimpy trip. As well as trying not to throw up every twenty minutes, I was anxious and edgy, as I always am before a mining town stint. I'm not sure why I get so wound up, but I think it's my fear of having left something behind or the stove on or that I haven't got enough ID to get past the check-in point. And I couldn't even drink before boarding, which usually helps ease the tension slightly. I'm fine once I get on the plane, but right up until they board us, I'm a little ball of anxiety. This could explain why I chose to break up with poor Dave before I left for Broome.

Pregnancy had brought out all of my doubts about our relationship. For the past year, I'd coped with my loneliness when Dave was working away by working in pubs, drinking in pubs and smoking weed (at home). All of my friends worked in the pub scene, and not many of them were interested in kids or pregnancy or talking about either subject (I don't blame them at all – I had zero interest myself until I got knocked up). Now I'd had a few weeks of sobriety and no social life, I was going batshit crazy.

It all came to a head when Dave drove me to the airport.

'When I come back from Broome I'm taking Chaos and going to live with Mum,' I announced out of the blue. I think I surprised myself as much as Dave with that statement. This just proves how crazy I was, because prior to this I never wanted to stay at Mum's for a single weekend, let alone on a more permanent basis.

'So you want to leave and have the baby on your own? What about me?'

Dave was not a 'sensitive new-age guy'. He was old school and didn't let little things like emotions get in his way. But I could see that he was upset about what I was saying. I wasn't purposely trying to hurt him, but I wasn't coping with the emotional rollercoaster that comes with being pregnant.

'You're never home. I'm sick of being so far from my family. I'm stuck out in Palmerston, I've got no friends and now I can't even work at the pub!'

This last part wasn't quite true – yet. At this stage the only thing bigger about me was my boobs and the boys weren't complaining at all, so I was still working behind the bar two or three afternoons a week at the Airport Tavern. But I knew I only had a few more weeks before my belly started to pop out.

'I'm out there working for you and the baby!' Dave, I could tell, was trying his best not to lose his shit but he was getting frustrated with me. This became obvious when we nearly ran into the car in front of us, which had stopped at a red light.

'Yeah, but you've been saying for the last year that you would move to Darwin, and you haven't even looked for a job here!'

'I'm flat out working in Gove! For fuck's sake, how am I supposed to find a job here when I'm over there? All my gear is in Gove. It'll cost a bomb to move across. You could help me find work, you know.'

'Oh yeah, right, cos I know all about driving machinery and roadworks. Sure I'll get you a job, Dave. Just don't complain if it's holding a stop sign!'

'Yeah, thanks, Kel, that's really fuckin' helpful.'

The light changed to green. We drove the rest of the way to the airport in silence. When I got out of the car, I barely said goodbye.

Trying to put the whole thing out of my mind, I bought a few magazines to read on the plane. Turned out that wasn't necessary. It was a small plane, which, as we all know, terrifies me, so I had enough to worry about that I managed to forget our argument for a while.

We made a short stop at Kununurra on the Northern Territory/Western Australia border, where half the passengers disembarked and the plane was refuelled (the fact that the plane was so small it couldn't get from Darwin to Broome on one tank of fuel did nothing to ease my worried mind). We flew on to Broome, where I was greeted by a bar manager from the pub I was booked into. She helped me carry my stuff to her car and gave me a lift into town.

As she drove, I took in my surroundings. It reminded me of Gove, probably due to the clear blue sky, red dust on the side of the road and the industrial buildings surrounding the airport. The town itself was not very big, the permanent population around 14,440, growing to about 45,000 in the tourist season. Broome was founded on the pearling industry and many of the original residents of the town were Chinese. To this day, Chinese culture still has a major presence in Broome. Of course, the town also has Aboriginal history and culture everywhere. They lived there a long time before the Chinese pearl divers.

The main street is only about a kilometre long but there are a few little shops and cafes as well as pearl museums,

'Chinatown' (an alleyway where most of the tourist shops are located), an old ice-cream parlour and the very first outdoor cinema in the country. It's definitely a holiday town, because the footpaths are lined with palm trees. Most of the people working in Broome are backpackers.

The Roebuck Hotel, or as the locals call it, The Roey, is a large old-style country pub in the heart of Broome. Actually, it pretty much *is* the heart of Broome. When I got there, the manager, who was also called Kelly, showed me to my room.

'Where's the other girl?' I asked her, thinking she'd be in the room already. I wasn't looking forward to sharing a room with a complete stranger for two weeks. There was a single bed and a double bed, which I thought was strange. Usually we girls shared rooms but they were tiny with two single beds and no bathroom. This room was a motel suite, bathroom and all.

'The other girl will be here in about an hour – she's flying in from Perth – but she'll be in the room next door.'

What? I got my own hotel room for two whole weeks? This place was amazing. And it got better.

'You have an allowance of one meal, either lunch or dinner, it's up to you. You can order anything on the menu.' Kelly smiled. 'You don't work Sundays but you still have a meal allowance – they have roast night on Sunday too, it's awesome.'

My eyes must have looked like saucers. 'So what you're saying is we get our own hotel room each, free food cooked to order and Sundays off?' I couldn't believe my ears. Most mining towns work you like a dog for two weeks, feed you scraps and accommodate you in a glorified kennel. This was going to be a walk in the park. Just my luck to get the best stint of my skimpy career just as I was about to end it – or at least take maternity leave from it!

After Kelly left, I showered and got ready for work. I'd recently bought a whole heap of new outfits cheaply from an online adult store. I highly recommend this because I saved about a thousand dollars. Most of the outfits were no more than twenty-five bucks each, so I managed to get one for nearly every day of the week. Tossing the costumes on the double bed, I started to try them on. I was like a little kid playing dress-ups, except all of the costumes were R-rated. I had a teeny little version of a witch's outfit, which came complete with a pointed hat, although after trying that on I decided to give the hat a miss; and a nurse's uniform that had a low-cut cleavage, which for once I could fill out, and a teensy little skirt that barely covered my butt. My latest favourite was a pirate costume with white billowy sleeves and a faux-leather corset-style dress, which, again, was so short it just skimmed the tops of my thighs and made me look like one of those beer wenches from Viking times. I decided to leave that for the weekend and went with the schoolgirl outfit, a one-piece minidress with a black skirt, tight, white low-cut shirt and suspenders over the shoulders. I did my hair in two plaits, slapped on some make-up and topped off the look with a large, chunky, fake-jewel-studded cross that I wore hanging from a chain around my neck. I looked a bit like Madonna, circa 1988.

I didn't meet my fellow skimpy, Ruby, until five minutes before our first shift. Ruby was twenty-one, with one of those edgy hairdos where some of her hair was long and the rest kind of shaved. She had a huge obsession with Marilyn Monroe and the tattoos to prove it. Her whole look was '50s rockabilly. Despite our age difference we got along straightaway. She had just started working in the industry and, like me, she loved the lifestyle that came with the job. We had both been to Kalgoorlie so we had that in common – although she didn't work at the pub Rhonda ran, so her experience was slightly better than the one I'd had.

We were working in the Oasis bar, a large old wooden semicircular bar with a small TAB room behind it. In the front was a huge function area with pool tables, leading out to a massive beer garden with palm trees scattered everywhere. After dark the beer garden turned into an outdoor nightclub, so there was a stage, where the entertainment ranged from live music to wet T-shirt competitions. We weren't allowed to enter the wet T-shirt competitions, though, as the pub said it wouldn't be fair. Apparently because of our job we had an 'advantage' over the other contestants. I didn't bother pointing out that most of the other girls I'd seen in the pub had heaps bigger boobs than me and that serving beer in your knickers doesn't make you more attractive in a wet T-shirt than anyone else. There isn't one part of me that wants to get up on stage in a wet T-shirt and be judged for it. Fuck that. I only parade around half naked if I'm getting paid.

We were to work from 3 to 7 p.m. each afternoon with an extra shift at lunchtime on Saturdays. It was different from Gove and Kalgoorlie because we weren't allowed to do 'jug runs'. We stayed fairly covered up and made hardly any tips. This time, though, I wasn't there for the money. I'd wanted to visit Broome for years, so as far as I was concerned it was an all-expenses-paid holiday. I wouldn't call our four-hour shifts behind the bar 'working hard'. From Monday to Wednesday it was pretty dead, with the largest crowd being around twenty people. It got busier in the second half of the week, but compared with other pubs I'd worked at it was still fairly relaxed.

Ruby and I ate dinner together every evening in the restaurant next door to the Oasis bar. It was here we met a group of blokes who were travelling around the country for the horse races. One of the guys owned racehorses and paid for his mates to join him on the competition circuit. Lucky bastards. They were in town for the Broome Cup. I was glad we met them, because poor Ruby had lucked out in terms of a partner in crime. I was in no condition to party all night. The most I could do was a wine with dinner. So while I was in bed by 10 p.m., at least Ruby had someone to party with, as the guys had a room right next to ours. There were also some backpackers working at the pub as barmaids and they all hung out together around the pool or in the beer garden. Yes, I was envious. Trust me to get knocked up just before a two-week stint in paradise. But I kept reminding myself that I had partied enough to rival Keith Richards when I was younger. A baby was more important than getting shit-faced and streaking down the main street.

I couldn't sit around in my room the whole time, though. I was still upset about the way I'd left Darwin and wondering what the hell Dave and I were going to do. We hadn't really spoken since he'd dropped me off at Darwin Airport. It was never my plan to be a single mother, but I had to admit to myself that I wasn't happy with the way things were. There didn't really seem to be an obvious solution. If I stayed with Dave, it meant I was isolated and bored. There was no way I was going to live in Gove, but moving closer to Mum meant the end of Dave and me. Argh! Why the fuck couldn't I have met a bloke with a normal nine-to-five job? Probably because he'd bore me to tears. Dave was a lot of things, but boring was not one of them.

Needing a distraction, I appointed myself tour guide and booked all kinds of touristy shit, which Ruby went along with. The poor bugger probably wanted to relax by the pool but instead I dragged her around Broome and forced her to participate in ridiculous activities like riding camels along a nudist beach.

The first Sunday we were there, a bloke we'd met at the bar offered to take us for a drive to the beaches around town. For the life of me I can't remember his name, so I'll just call him Curly, because he had black curly hair. He took us out in a reliable version of Dave's troopy. We were headed out of town, flying along red-dirt roads, when it crossed my mind that no one would hear us scream.

Luckily for us, Curly turned out not to be a serial killer. When we arrived at James Price Point, we saw a large hippie camp. The hippies were protesting about a gas plant that was proposed to be built in the sea, just off the point. Their sign read 'You can't put a price on the Point', which I thought was rather catchy. Beyond the hippies was a spectacular view. Red rocky cliffs and sand looked amazing next to the turquoise-blue water. My camera battery was dead so it was bloody lucky Ruby had hers. We drove along the beach and collected shells and rocks, channelling our inner five-year-olds. Bravely, I even dipped my big toe in the water.

Here's the thing I don't get about Broome. It's nearly as far north as Darwin, but the locals seem to think there are no crocs in the water. A few blokes at the pub told me they had one croc in town and it lived in a saltwater creek, apparently never venturing away from its home. Now call me paranoid, but I don't trust crocodiles and I don't trust the water that surrounds the top part of Australia. I also don't believe for one second that the croc didn't leave its territory. Crocodiles are predators and predators are always hunting for food. So I wasn't game to test the local theory that the beach was croc-free. And it seemed I wasn't being paranoid after all. Not so long ago there was a four-metre salty spotted surfing the waves at Cable Beach.

During the next week we discovered pearl-diving museums, markets and quirky shops, and spent a couple of evenings at the outdoor cinema. I booked us in for a sunset camel ride on Broome's famous Cable Beach. When I mentioned this to the locals, they were like, 'What the hell do you want to ride a camel for? You should go and visit the croc farm.' And I would reply, 'I live in Darwin, mate; I'm not paying to look at a bloody crocodile.'

So on our last Sunday evening we took the bus from the pub to Cable Beach, which is a stunning combination of blue skies and water and soft white sand. The tour guides took us to a grumpy-looking camel named Isaac, who stank like a urinal. He didn't look too stoked to be there. Oh well, it was too late now. I'd paid my money and I wasn't leaving without a photo of me on the bloody animal.

Ruby and I climbed up on top of Isaac, her sitting in the saddle behind me. The camels, who were all joined together in a kind of conga line, started their trek down the beach. Along the way we spotted several nudists (Cable Beach is also a well-known nudie hotspot). As usual, the people baring all in public were the ones who probably shouldn't, but it was fun playing 'spot the nudist' with Ruby.

Twenty minutes into our ride, I was over it. This was literally a pain in the arse! I felt sorry for anyone who relied on camels as their main form of transport. I got my picture, though: a professional photo of Ruby, Isaac and me with the sunset in the background. Every time I look at it my bum hurts.

The next morning I flew back to Darwin. As soon as I saw Dave at the airport, I realised how much I'd missed him.

Maybe I had been too quick to throw it all away. He wrapped me up in a big bear hug.

I looked up at him. 'I'm sorry I was such a bitch. I'm just so lonely up here.'

'I know y'are, Kel.' He patted me on the back. 'But I can't do much about it. I can't make friends for you.'

'Yeah, I know,' I sighed.

'As soon as I can get onto a good job over here I promise I'll move over and you won't have to be on your own.'

'I hope so,' I said. I'd decided over the last two weeks that I owed it to our baby to give it a go. So, for now, I was sticking around.

Wanting to give our relationship the best chance possible, I decided it might be a good idea to see a counsellor to work through the different emotions that come with pregnancy and the stress of being on my own for most of it.

I'm not a person who loves talking about my feelings. Most of the time I just like to chuck it in the fuck-it bucket and move on. Opening up to a complete stranger is the last thing I want to do. But after a couple of sessions I started to get comfortable enough to confide in her.

It was halfway through my fourth session – while I was confiding my innermost feelings – that she interrupted me.

'Is that today's *NT News*?' she asked.

Completely baffled as to what this had to do with what I was saying, I replied, 'Um … Yes, it is.'

'Oh, can I please have a quick look?' she said.

Now I was really wondering what the fuck was going on.

'Right now? I can leave it for you to read after the session if you like,' I said.

'No, no that's fine,' she said. 'I just want to have a look at the classifieds – I need a new wardrobe.'

I didn't know what to say to that. I mean, I know I talk a lot but this person was getting *paid* to listen. If counsellors are supposed to help with self-esteem issues, it was a funny way to go about it! I handed the paper over in disbelief.

She opened it up and started browsing. I should have got up and walked out but, no, I sat there feeling like a fuckwit until she finished reading. Once she was satisfied there were no suitable wardrobes for sale that day, she put the paper down and smiled at me.

'So, what were you saying?'

I never went back after that.

CHAPTER 14

ADULT ENTERTAINMENT

WHEN I FIRST ARRIVED IN DARWIN, AS WELL as working in pubs I did a couple of jobs for an 'agency' that turned out to be nothing more than a front for an ex-stripper with an ice habit and a list of criminal convictions as long as a roll of toilet paper. I stopped working for her after I realised she was taking more than 50 per cent commission out of my pay.

To get more work, I decided to freelance and started advertising myself as a skimpy in the local classifieds. Between this and the contacts I was making at the pub, after a while I had more and more blokes calling me, requesting a skimpy for all kinds of functions, from golf days to Christmas parties. I couldn't do every job myself so I ended up booking other girls for some of the jobs. I had met lots of girls through working at pubs and freelancing. I'd often get girls contacting me via my advert to work with them on a job they had been asked to do, and before long I had a great network in Darwin. So it wasn't hard to fill the jobs as they came in. It was pretty much what I used to do at the Gold Coast agency I'd worked for but on a much smaller scale. I didn't make much money out of it but it was fun. I'd forgotten how much I loved the challenge of finding the best girls for the job and how satisfying it was when you got a call from the blokes saying how great the night went.

I was also happy I could provide work for the girls and entertainment for the customers without ripping anyone off. I didn't take money out of the girls' fees and I didn't charge the customer a ridiculous booking fee either. Dave would tell me I was ripping myself off, but after being ripped off by the dodgy agency I'd first worked for in Darwin, I was determined to make sure that my prices were fair and the girls were happy with what I was paying. After all, they were the ones showing up and doing the work. Charging the customers $60 per hour in commission was daylight robbery as far as I was concerned. I wasn't going to operate that way.

So, for now, as much as I hated to admit it, booking adult entertainment seems to be my calling. After paying private school fees for my first three years of high school, I'm sure my parents are delighted.

When I got back from Broome, it was time to finish up my work at the Airport Tavern. I was now about thirteen weeks pregnant; the pregnancy was going well, with my three-month scan showing a very healthy baby, and I was starting to get rounder in the tummy. When I told the manager I was leaving, he wasn't thrilled. It's not that I was the world's best barmaid but at least he knew I would show up. Dealing with the skimpies drove him nuts, and I couldn't blame him. I knew only too well how unreliable some girls could be. And he had an entire pub to run; he really didn't need the stress of finding skimpy staff and dealing with no-shows. So I offered to do it for him. We agreed that I would find girls for the skimpy shifts and be responsible for their wages and roster. I was more than happy with this arrangement. I knew that once I stopped working I'd go nuts with boredom, especially when Dave was out working for two- to three-week stints.

I don't know why I thought I would stay sane managing skimpies again. I must have forgotten all those times I practically had to beg girls to turn up for work and to calm down angry pub owners when they didn't show up, despite my bribes and threats of no more work. I had some fantastic girls working behind the bar most of the time, but I also had some shockers. At first I was all sweetness and light with them but eventually I toughened up. I had no choice. Girls would invoice me for shifts they hadn't shown up for, or call in 'sick' an hour before their shift.

One girl sent me a text an hour or two before she was supposed to be at work: *I'm sorry I can't work today I have laryngitis.* I'd had laryngitis in the past and knew how important it is to rest your voice, so I sent her back a text telling her not to worry about work and to get better. Later that night I was scrolling through my Facebook feed and who did I see lying beside a pool with what looked suspiciously like a cocktail in her hand? Yep, little Miss Laryngitis! I sent her a message asking why she would be at a pool party when she was supposed to be sick. Her answer? She thought it would help her feel better.

Another girl who worked in the bar at the Airport Tavern for a few weeks sent me an email saying I hadn't paid an invoice of hers. I checked the date against my paperwork and I had in fact paid her. I emailed her the reference number and she sent back a message saying it must have been some other date and I would need to look back and find this so-called missing invoice. I pointed out that it actually wasn't my job to chase up her paperwork and that I couldn't find any missing invoice without an invoice number or a date. She sent back a very angry email threatening to take me to the Department of Fair Trading, to which my reply was: what are you going to tell them? That I owe you money for an invoice you can't provide and can't give dates for? Good luck with that. Funnily enough, I never heard from her again.

Not everyone tried to swindle me, however. I've ended up mates with a few of the girls I've had working in the bar. These days I'm better at picking reliable skimpies and generally prefer girls who have been in the industry for a few years and treat it like a proper job. Nothing annoys me more than a girl not showing up when she says she will because she thinks the job is optional. What they don't realise is the pub needs them to show up or the blokes will walk out. And at $60 an hour I couldn't understand why they would want to cancel. I was still showing up when I was struggling with morning sickness so I had little sympathy for girls who cancelled at the last minute due to a sudden 'illness' (more like a hangover).

I'm sure there are a few girls out there who would happily stick a knife in my back these days. But if an ex-barmaid has a problem with me, it's usually because I had to sack her for failing to show up. In one case a girl did show up but brought her boyfriend, who happened to be a complete psycho. He sat at the bar watching her while she worked, then after her shift they took off in his car, doing burnouts in the pub's car park. Then, probably disorientated due to all that spinning, they crashed the car through the fence surrounding the car park. They drove off, taking half the fence home with them. Obviously the pub didn't want her back after that.

It was difficult to sack a girl I hardly knew, but even worse when I was friends with her. That has only happened once but it was awful.

I'd met Nicole when she was pregnant but still working behind the bar as a skimpy at another Darwin pub. Most women start showing at about three months, but Nicole was like me and could hide the bump well into her fourth month of pregnancy. After that it gets a bit hard to hide, and skimpy work is not for pregnant women. Unless you count the topless girl at the Noonamah pub, about sixty kilometres out of town, who worked right up until she gave birth. But Noonamah is remote so it's hard to get girls to drive out there, and I think the guys were just happy to look at a pair of boobs, belly or no belly. Anyway, I'd worked with Nicole a few times and she was always great behind the bar. She's very petite (her nickname is Pixie) with blonde hair and a bubbly personality. The guys loved her, other girls got on well with her and she worked hard – no one ever had an empty glass in their hand when Nicole was working. After she left and had her baby we stayed in touch, so when it was my turn to go on 'maternity leave' she was one of the first people I thought of to work behind the bar at the Airport

Tavern. She'd got her figure back quickly and was ready to get back to work.

I have no idea why but for some reason the customers at the Airport didn't take to her the way they did at the last pub she worked at. It happens – sometimes girls get along better with different crowds – but this was awkward because she was also my friend. Unfortunately that didn't matter and the pub told me she wasn't to come back. I had to break the news and obviously she was upset. Not with me; she told me she understood that while the news was shit I was just doing my job. But I didn't realise just how pissed off she was with the pub.

She decided to take her grievances to the local newspaper. The night before the article came out she called to let me know, assuring me it wasn't a big deal. Probably just a tiny article a couple of paragraphs long on the third or fourth page, she reckoned.

The next day, on the front page of the *NT News*, there was my friend, topless, in a pair of pink lacy knickers, sitting on a beer keg with a tray of drinks covering her boobs. You couldn't see her face but you could see her blonde hair. The headline read: 'TOPLESS BARMAID CANNED'.

Oh, fuck. My first reaction was to call the pub. I asked to speak to the manager, who I was sure was going to tear me a new one. 'It's Kel, I'm so sorry. She did mention she had spoken to the paper but I had no idea it was going to be a front-page story!'

'Don't worry about it, mate,' he said. 'It's great advertising for the pub!'

Phew. So I wasn't in trouble there. My next call was to Nicole. 'Mate, what the fuck? I thought you said they were doing a small article, not the front bloody page!'

'Kel, I'm sorry, I had no idea they'd make such a big deal. I didn't say half of what was written. I was pissed off with the pub but I didn't mean to get you into any trouble.'

After my 'Darwin or Bust' story with the same paper, I knew how she felt.

Nicole might not have got her job back at the Airport but she did get some great photos out of it. These days we can look back on the whole thing and laugh. She's now working at the pub where we met and has no hard feelings towards the Airport Tavern any more. In fact, if I'm ever short-staffed (which happens more often than I'd like), she's one of the first people to try to help me find someone to fill the shift. She tells me I'm crazy for getting back into the admin side of the industry. A few years earlier she had operated an agency in Darwin before deciding that dealing with unreliable girls wasn't worth the stress involved. She much preferred to work at the party herself, instead of organising it for them. I have moments when I wonder myself why I'm doing it. The only answer I can come up with is that no matter how frustrating it gets, it's never boring.

CHAPTER 15

MAYHEM MEETS CHAOS

AT TWENTY WEEKS PREGNANT, I WENT FOR a routine check-up and was given the choice to be told the baby's sex. I didn't want to wait another twenty weeks to find out, so I chose to know then.

I was sure it was going to be a boy. Dave didn't have an opinion on the matter either way, but I'd already picked out a name: Thomas Anthony, after Dave's father and mine. So it came as a bit of a shock when, as I was lying on the hospital bed with cold goo all over my belly, the sonographer told me he was 99 per cent sure I was having a girl.

'Are you positive?' I asked him.

'Yep, it's usually pretty easy to tell when it comes to females,' he told me.

'Shit,' I said to Dave, who was sitting next to the bed. 'I wasn't expecting this … We can't call a girl Thomas.' I had my heart set on that name and really hadn't prepared myself for the possibility that I was having a girl.

'We can call her Davina,' replied Dave.

'Over my dead body,' I shot back.

After a couple of days I got used to the idea and realised that I was actually pretty bloody excited to be having a girl. A little mini Kel. The house was too male dominated anyway, between Chaos and Dave. It would be nice having another girl around the place.

One day at the end of September 2012, while I was sitting around at home growing fatter, Dave called from work. 'Kel, remember my mate Jim? You know, the one with the Flintstones house?'

'Yeah, how could I forget?' I replied. We had visited Jim a few months earlier at his house in a little town called Darwin River just before he moved down to New South Wales to be with his new girlfriend. He was quite a character, and the house looked like it had been built out of rocks, cement and probably a whole heap of material stolen from building sites.

'He's got no one living in his house at the moment and wants to know if we would be keen on movin' into the joint.'

Was the Pope a Catholic? Do bears shit in the woods? I'd have moved there that afternoon if I could. The place might have been built from whatever Jim could get his hands on for little or no money, but it was out on a fifty-acre property and about ten kilometres up the road from my favourite swimming hole, Berry Springs.

The house itself wasn't too bad despite the fact that it was a glorified shed. Jim had rendered the inside walls to give it a cave-like effect, and the kitchen was huge, separated from the lounge room and main bedroom by big glass sliding doors, which allowed the lounge room to stay cool while leaving the kitchen completely open. There was a front and back veranda and the house was surrounded by large trees, tropical palms and perfectly maintained landscaped gardens (which surprised me, considering the state of the house). The bathroom was under the back veranda and it was also built out of cement and rocks, keeping the cave theme going. There were about five tree frogs living in the shower and a cane toad usually cowering in the corner. The toilet was also outdoors and it was pretty open, meaning that you could sit on the loo and enjoy a great sunset view of the paddocks with flies buzzing around your head, a dog trying to climb on your lap and a frog up your arse. The frogs lived *inside* the loo as well as the shower and every now and then you would have one trying to climb out while you were doing your business.

Despite all of this — or, more accurately, because of all this — I jumped at the opportunity to move out there. I didn't really need to be in town as I'd be leaving the radio job soon (the morning sickness had gone way past four months: I was struggling to sound bubbly at 7 a.m. when really all I wanted to do was lie next to the loo with a cold washer and some soda water) and my new role managing the skimpies at the Airport Tavern could be done from home.

We moved out to the property a couple of weeks later — and when I say 'we' moved, I mean Dave and his workmate Ben moved all the stuff while I watched them. Being pregnant can really suck so I took any opportunity to get some perks out of the situation. Besides, it was the beginning of the 'build-up', the hottest, muggiest time of year up in Darwin, and at five and a half months pregnant with morning sickness until at least 10 a.m., I was about as useful as the proverbial tits on a bull. The boys did a great job and I did my bit by buying them rum and cooking them dinner afterwards. Well, actually, I didn't quite cook: I bought a barbecued chicken, some salad and bread rolls, but the point is they got fed.

I had been looking forward to moving out to the property despite the isolation, as it was another dream of mine to live on a 'farm'. I was distracted by all the stuff I had to do out there to get ready for the baby, and Dave and I had started talking about moving either back over to Queensland or to coastal New South Wales. Dave was also still going on about moving over to Darwin first then leaving the Territory. To be honest, I never knew what the fuck he was really thinking half the time when it came to where we were going to live. It was frustrating and I didn't feel I had a lot of control over it. Most of the time I spent up in the Territory I was just trying to make the best of a less than ideal living situation. The flat in Gove wasn't big enough for all of us, the Palmerston unit was slightly better but still not where I wanted to spend the rest of my life, and now we were living in a shed. I just went with it.

Shortly after we moved into our new home, Mayhem arrived. Literally. Our new American staffy cross pup, Mayhem, or Maisie for short, was part of my plan to help Chaos deal with the little Gumnut, as I had nicknamed my bump. I'd discussed with Dave how I was going to get Chaos used to living outside and not being the centre of my world any more. We figured that if he had another dog around it would be company for him and distract him from being jealous of the baby. It didn't quite work out like that at first, though. Chaos wasn't at all happy about Maisie's arrival. He wasn't aggressive towards her but would simply walk out of the room if she walked in. If she tried to play with him he'd turn away from her or get up and move. I was convinced he would never accept her. But within two weeks I caught him being nice to her in the garden while he thought no one was looking. For some reason if he knew I was there he'd go back to being a total arsehole to her again. I felt sorry for her but she didn't seem to mind. Once she got a bit bigger she started lording it over him so much that I began to feel sorry for him instead. She adored Chaos and had to be practically on top of him at all times. The poor bastard had no privacy any more and his bed was no longer his own. She seemed to take up the best part of it and I'd often find him lying on the concrete next to it, having given up on the idea of getting his bed to himself ever again.

Chaos wasn't the only one who had to adapt to a new house guest. Living in the middle of the bush means you have to be prepared to share your accommodation with the local wildlife. The night we moved in, we had an English bloke staying there who'd been looking after the place for Jim while he had no one living in it. He'd been there for a few weeks and gave me some tips to help me settle in. 'At night, you might hear a few strange noises, but don't worry, it's just the possums in the roof, nothing to worry about. It's definitely not a ghost or anything,' he explained to me over dinner that night. I just looked at him with an amused expression on my face and went along with it. He obviously had no idea that I knew the backstory to that particular piece of advice.

The story goes, as Jim had told Dave and me earlier, that after the Pommy's first couple of nights staying at the house alone he called Jim, sounding a tiny bit stressed. 'Mate, there's some weird noises in the roof at night, I can't figure out what it is … it's got me a bit worried.'

'Oh yeah, don't worry about that. There was an old bloke living in the shed there before me; he died in the place, and he moves around a bit at night,' Jim lied.

Our Pommy friend freaked right out. 'What the fuck? Mate, are you serious?'

'He won't bother you, just put some earplugs in and try not to piss him off, I s'pose.'

After about a week Jim must have felt sorry for the guy and told him the truth – that the only things that had died in that house were cane toads and bush rats – because here he was, reassuring me that there were definitely no ghosts on the property.

To be honest, sometimes I would have preferred to share the house with a grumpy old ghost than the wildlife I seemed to be tripping over from the moment I got out of bed. I felt like Dr Dolittle. I'd have a shower with an audience of five tree frogs and one cane toad at my feet. He became my little shower buddy. He'd hear me coming and hop to the corner and I would make sure I stuck to my half of the shower. Soon enough it became perfectly normal.

It was also perfectly normal to be walking down the driveway, minding your own business, when out of nowhere a python crossed in front of you. They didn't bother me too much because they weren't close to the house, but I was still paranoid about them finding their way inside.

Jim had told me a story that made my hair stand on end the way no ghost could. He was asleep in the lounge room on a beanbag when he woke to see a pair of reptile eyes staring straight at him. A snake had slithered through a hole in the roof and was now upright in attack mode, watching for Jim's next move. He grabbed the snake by the throat and chucked it outside. Not how I would have dealt with the situation, but Jim is the epitome of rough outback bushman. A couple of his mates reckoned they took him out hunting and he found a three-day-old iced coffee under the passenger seat of the car they were in. He opened it up and drank it, lumps and all. His mates vomited just watching him drink it, but Jim didn't see a problem. A little thing like a snake in the lounge room wasn't going to rattle him.

I nearly had an encounter with a snake of a different kind when Chaos went wandering one afternoon. I'd let him off the chain to have a play in the garden while I hung washing on the line and watered the plants. It was about thirty-five degrees and as humid as ever. Being nearly six months pregnant made it even worse, so all I had on was a pair of knickers. I didn't need to worry about anyone catching me walking around half naked, though. On one side of the property was a nudist retreat and on the other a buffalo farm. So, when you think about it, I was actually overdressed.

As I wandered around the yard I called out to Chaos, and when he didn't come after five minutes I started to fear the worst. He loves nothing more than a good old cattle chase, and buffalo don't fuck around. The horns on those things are, like, a metre long. If he was in the paddock next door, he was probably going to doggy heaven.

I didn't have time to get dressed; I chucked on a bra and some sneakers and ran down the back paddock, yelling out for my dog.

'CHAOS! WHERE THE BLOODY HELL ARE YOU?' I half ran, half waddled down the paddock. My belly had popped out quite a bit by now and everything I did made me look like a penguin.

'What's going on?' I heard a voice call out from behind the bushes on the other side of our fence, the nudist side.

'Hang on! Don't come over, I'm only in my bra and undies!' I answered without thinking. Next thing I knew, a naked woman emerged from the scrub where the voice had come from. I'd forgotten in my panic that clothes were optional around these parts. Everyone thinks living next door to nudists would be great, but I'm here to tell you once again that the people who love going nude are usually the ones who shouldn't. They're not exactly supermodels, and this sixty-year-old woman standing in front of me was no exception. She was a very lovely person, though.

'It's all right, love, my husband found your dog and just took him down to the gate so he could get back onto your property.'

Oh, great. Another naked person.

'That's really nice of you guys,' I thanked her as we both walked along the fence-line dividing our property from theirs, towards her husband and Chaos. Just two women walking together, one in her underwear and one in her birthday suit. I was hoping to see Chaos before the husband and get the hell out of there. I really didn't want to have to deal with a sixty-year-old naked man as well. For once, luck was on my side, and at the point where we met up with her husband the grass growing on the fence-line was so tall that any snakes in the area were well and truly hidden.

CHAPTER 16

KEL VS THE STUART HIGHWAY
- PART II -

ON A MUGGY AFTERNOON IN LATE OCTOBER 2012, the buffalo grazing in their paddocks were startled by a huge commotion from the house next door.

'You want me to pay twelve hundred bucks to fly two dogs to Melbourne? Are you bloody kidding me?' I ranted to the woman on the other end of the phone who was currently ruining my life. 'I've never paid more than a hundred bucks to fly a dog interstate; I've even flown him into bloody Arnhem Land! Why are you charging so much?'

'Because you didn't book the dogs onto the flight when you booked your ticket, there is no room for them and they must go on another flight,' the operator told me. 'So that means you must pay for them as cargo, not extra baggage.'

So it was my fault.

First the lady at the boarding kennels had told me that I should have booked in July if I wanted the dogs looked after over the Christmas holidays. Now this bloody woman from the airline was telling me that if I wanted to bring them on my holiday I should've booked them on the plane with me in the first place. When I booked my flight to Melbourne for Christmas, I had just assumed I would get them into boarding kennels. But in the laid-back town of Darwin, the only thing people actually plan ahead for, it seems, is holiday time. Every dog kennel in the area was booked out, even the crap ones that use shipping containers instead of actual dog pens. And the kennel owners didn't help by sounding smug when they told me I had left it too late. I don't know why they took pleasure in my misery. Maybe living on a property with a hundred howling dogs had made them a tad miserable themselves so they were happy to have company every now and then. Who knows? What I did know was that now it looked like I was stuck in Darwin River, which was so freaking hot it was beginning to feel like the fiery pits of hell.

I looked out the window at the Suzuki Swift hatchback parked in the driveway. It was nineteen years old but ran all right. Put it this way, the axles all stayed in place and the brakes hadn't failed yet. There was no reason why I couldn't drive it down to Albury with the dogs in the back. I'd originally planned to fly to Melbourne then catch the train up to Albury from there. Why not leave a few weeks early and drive down? I thought. What else was I going to do while Dave was away working? It was so humid and sticky, the only thing I could do during the day was lie next to the airconditioner looking like a carpet snake that had swallowed a sheep.

I called Mum with the good news. She was thrilled that I was coming down earlier, but didn't want me driving all that way. 'Kel, there's a lady on my Facebook page who lives in Darwin; I could see if she can look after the dogs or knows someone who can and then you can fly down,' she suggested.

'Thanks, Mum, but seriously, Darwin River is seventy kilometres from Darwin – no one will want to drive out here twice a day to feed them and walk them. It's okay, I'm actually starting to get excited about this road trip. This time I'll have a CD player and can afford motels. It'll be fun!'

I wasn't just saying it for Mum's benefit. Road trips are what I live for. If I wasn't such a questionable driver, I'd definitely drive road trains for a living. Maybe once I can reverse-park a car without breaking all the side mirrors, I'll think about getting my truck licence.

'Kel, I'm really worried about you driving down on your own – you're six months pregnant, you're going to get tired and it's a long way.'

You'd think I had just told her I'd entered the New York Marathon. 'Mum, I'll be doing the trip over five days; it's really not as bad as it sounds.' I tried to reassure her by breaking the trip down. 'Just think of it this way – "today Kel's driving to Tennant Creek, tomorrow she's driving to Alice Springs, and the day after she'll drive to Coober Pedy" … not "oh my god, she's driving all the way from Darwin to Albury!"'

After about half an hour of this, Mum started to accept that I had made up my mind – or so I thought. The next few days were peppered with concerned phone calls from my grandmother, sister and aunty, all of whom lived in Melbourne and thought I was insane. Nothing could change my mind, though – I had the stubbornness and determination of my buffalo neighbours once I put my mind to something. Eventually, instead of pointing out the million and one things that could go wrong, they accepted that I was going to do this whether or not it was the stupidest thing they'd ever heard.

I spent the next two weeks getting the car ready and planning my drive. Last time I had done the Darwin to Albury trip it had been a last-minute decision with no time to plan anything except a basic route. This time I researched accommodation along the Stuart Highway and booked ahead so that I didn't get stuck sleeping on the side of the road again. I don't think the Swift would have been as comfy as the old troopy.

SKIMPY

Around the same time as I was planning my trip, the radio station Triple J was running a competition in conjunction with ABC Open over the summer months called the Road Trip Relay. People all over Australia could participate, and the idea was that every major road in the country would be covered. They wanted people to take pictures and submit stories as they drove. The prizes were pretty cool, including a $200 camera, so I thought why the hell not? I entered my Stuart Highway trip into the comp and was contacted by a producer from ABC Open asking me to document my trip on video and convert it to 'time lapse'. They would then edit it in with other footage submitted by road trippers to make one giant road-trip film covering different roads all over the country. I tried to tell them that my technical skills weren't my strong point but they didn't care. They only had two other entrants who were driving the Stuart Highway when I entered so they were pretty keen for me to do this.

One of the ladies I spoke to at ABC Darwin talked me through the process, and although I was still a bit worried about my ability to pull it off, I went ahead and agreed to do it. Dave attached the video camera to the dashboard of my car with velcro and I bought a memory card with a million megabytes in it to record the length of the Stuart Highway, from Darwin in the Territory to Port Augusta in South

Australia, which is 2724 kilometres. It was going to be a long bloody movie.

I decided that if I was going to do this trip and enter this comp I should get right into the spirit of things and promote the relay a bit as I drove through the outback. Inspired by the movie *The Adventures of Priscilla, Queen of the Desert*, which I had just recently rewatched, I contacted a local Darwin company, Gecko Signs, and asked them to help me jazz up my car. The owners were almost as excited about the trip as I was and we worked together to get the Swift ready for its journey. I ended up with big shiny stickers that said 'Queen of the Desert' emblazoned all over my car. The stickers reflected the sunlight and you would have been able to see them from an aeroplane. Dave took one look at it and swore he'd never be seen in the car again. It would be pretty hilarious to see a bloke his size, with the big beard and crazy curly hair, driving a tiny little girl's car with 'Queen of the Desert' written all over it.

On 13 November I put Chaos and Mayhem into the back seat of the Suzuki and Dave checked all my emergency gear for the four hundredth time. He had the boot jam-packed with tyre-changing kits, battery packs, torches, fuel and water. I barely had room for luggage. Luckily, because I was pregnant, all I really needed was about five maxidresses and enough knickers to see me through to Albury. Then

I'd buy more clothes down there, because even though they thought it was hot down south, I knew I'd need some warmer clothes. Southerners don't know humidity until they've experienced a Darwin build-up. I was so used to the heat by now that I'd start shivering at any temperature below twenty-seven degrees.

Finally, I sat my pregnant arse in the driver's seat, kissed Dave goodbye and took off down the driveway, Dave waving behind me until I couldn't see him any more.

I made it all the way to the Berry Springs local servo before I made my first stop – I'd driven about ten kilometres. After filling up the hatchback and shouting myself a bacon and egg roll that drove the dogs insane while I was eating it, I headed off again, this time making it all the way to Mataranka before stopping. The last time I'd been here was when I lost my keys at the park where I'd camped. This time I was just driving through, as I planned to stay the night at Tennant Creek, about a thousand kilometres south of Darwin. I stopped anyway, to take some photos of the pub, hoping to find a local person to interview for the Road Trip Relay. I headed inside and took some photos of the little wooden bar and the old newspaper articles pinned up on the walls, right next to a calendar featuring my mate Phil O'Brien. I took a few photos to send to him so he could see how famous he is in the NT. I couldn't find the bar staff, who I figured were probably also the cleaners, yardies and owners of the place, the way they are in most outback pubs.

Wanting to get back on the road as quickly as possible, I left the pub and stood outside on the footpath, scouting around for someone to interview. Finally I spotted two men who were sitting in a tip truck that had an excavator loaded on the back. One of the blokes, the younger of the two, had climbed down from the cabin of the truck and was heading my way, towards the pub.

'Hey, mate,' I called out. 'Can I just do a quick interview with you? I'm doing it for this competition Triple J has on at the moment ...' I added, thinking that if I mentioned Triple J he'd be pretty keen; most young people listen to the station. He just looked at me blankly and said okay. He had an accent and looked to be of either Greek or Italian descent, but I didn't think that would be too much of a problem as there were a fair few backpackers living and working in the outback. Although his offsider looked a bit old to be joining in on Contiki tours, but who was I to judge? Anyway, I was desperate to get an interview and get the fuck out of there, so any human being capable of answering a few questions would do. I was too pregnant and hot to give a shit what the actual answers were.

Turns out it's a bit hard to interview someone who barely speaks a word of English. The interview went something like this:

'G'day, mate, how ya going?' I asked him, then, to the camera, 'So we're in Mataranka and I've met this local – what's your name, mate?'

He said something but I didn't catch it. 'It's what, sorry?'

'Zoran,' he said, a bit louder this time.

'Oh, Zoran, okay, and how long have you been in Mataranka for?'

'I don't understand,' he said with a confused grin.

'How long have you lived in Mataranka for?' I repeated.

'Uh, I still don't understand.'

'How long have you lived here?' I said, gesturing around the town.

'Oh, here? One year.'

'A year?' I checked that I'd understood him properly. He nodded. 'And what do you guys do for fun in Mataranka?'

He looked at me blankly again.

'What do you guys do for fun, you know, when you're not workin'?'

'Oh, not working? Go to Sydney,' he said.

'Ah, you go to Sydney, okay, so you don't get on the piss at this pub here? Nup?'

Zoran just smiled and shrugged, clueless as to what I'd just said.

'All right, mate, thanks for ya time, we'll let you go and, yeah, good old Mataranka, hey?' As you can probably tell I had no script planned and was just talking shit by this stage, especially as my Mataranka mate wasn't exactly making it easy for me. But I had done what I planned to do, which was interview someone who lived in Mataranka.

So I was a bit surprised to see them a few hours later on the road, several hundred kilometres from Mataranka, heading in the same direction as I was. After pulling up at the same truck stop, I had to find out where they were headed.

'Oi! You two! Where are ya headed now? Are you stalking me or what?' I asked them in my polite, ladylike manner.

'We headed to Sydney,' the older guy said in his thick Mediterranean accent.

'Oh, right. Geez, that's a long way from Mataranka, do you have family there?' I asked him.

'No, we live in Sydney. We go home.'

'So you don't actually live in Mataranka then?' I felt like a bit of a dingbat at this stage. Why would a backpacker be driving around in a garbage truck with his dad (I assumed the old bloke was his father)? I mean, who would invite their father along on a Contiki tour? Talk about having a blonde

The view from the world's smallest plane – flying across East Arnhem Land to Ramingining. It was around this point that I realised that whether I liked it or not, I was well and truly stuck there for as long as it would take Dave to fix the road.

Ramo airport – the height of sophistication out in the NT scrub.

No matter how many times they were warned not to drive to the boat ramp, the lure of barramundi was too strong to keep the local anglers from trying. On another note, if you ever need spare parts for your 4WD, they are everywhere out here.

My view from Dave's lap as he attempted to fix the boggy mess. He kicked me out soon after because apparently I was a distraction.

The tree frogs came out for a perv every time I got in the shower.

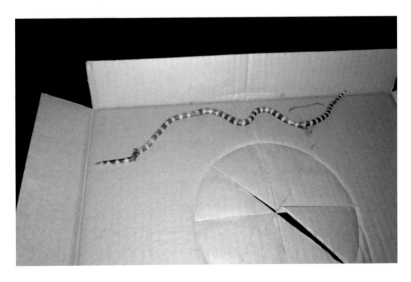

The psychotic bandy-bandy – or, as Dave likes to call it, the earthworm. Despite what he says, that thing was out to kill me.

Before my first shift at the Roebuck
Hotel, Broome.

Twenty-nine years old, knocked up
and representing one of the biggest
car races in Australia – only in the
Territory.

Got his rum and smokes – happy days! Dave chills out at Litchfield
National Park.

Firing up the engine to take on the Stuart Highway for a second lap.

After four days on the road I was going a bit crazy, as you can tell by this pic taken at Kulgera Roadhouse, the first or last pub in the NT depending on which way you were headed.

The desert is full of crazy shit like this – that's why I love it so much. I haven't seen a UFO yet, but then I haven't taken LSD in the middle of the desert either – I think there could be a connection.

Dave channelling his inner Captain Jack Sparrow – he does remind me of a crazy pirate.

Dave taking a tilt at Daddy Daycare.

Despite my fear of small planes, I was that bored in Gove I decided to get on a flight anyway – in the cockpit!

Jim Jim Falls, Kakadu – having a snooze after a long hike. When I woke up I found yowie footprints, although Dave didn't agree with me.

moment! I didn't mention any of this when I submitted the video. It was too late to turn around and get a real local on film so I just pretended that was how it is in Mataranka and left it at that. Probably one of the reasons why I didn't end up winning the grand prize. Which wasn't too disappointing, considering the grand prize was a bunch of photography equipment that I would have had no idea how to use.

My next interview went much better. I stopped in at the Larrimah Wayside Inn, home to a giant Pink Panther that is perched on the side of the road next to a giant NT stubby. They have a mini zoo out the back of the pub and I managed to track down one of the staff who work with the animals and talk her into doing an interview with me. She was my sort of chick too, a really down-to-earth country woman with a no-bullshit attitude. She chatted to the camera about the birds, snakes and crocs that live at the pub, and I joked that having a salty on the premises must be a good incentive for the pub clientele to behave themselves. After a shaky start, I was finally getting the hang of this whole interviewing thing. In fact, I was starting to wonder if I should contact *60 Minutes* and apply for a job.

After talking a German tourist into taking a photo of me sitting on the Pink Panther's lap, it was time to get cracking. Tennant Creek was still a fair hike and I didn't want to drive through the outback after dark in a car the size of a matchbox. Some of the roos that hopped across the road at night-time were bigger than the bloody car. And then you also have to worry about wandering cattle, because the Stuart Highway runs through huge cattle stations and none of them are fenced in. Meaning you could quite easily hit a cow at 130 kilometres an hour if you were in the wrong place at the wrong time.

I rolled into Tennant Creek about 7 p.m. I'd knocked a thousand kilometres off my trip, and I was pretty happy with that, especially since I'd stopped to do two interviews ... even if one of them was a bit on the strange side. Tennant Creek, which is smack bang in the middle of the outback, has quite the reputation as one of the roughest towns in the desert. As much as I hated to let fear get in my way, I was a bit nervous about staying there alone, even with one and a half pit bulls (Maisie wasn't scaring anyone yet). I found my hotel at the end of the main street and was relieved to see that they had big iron gates at the front – I don't think they locked us in at night, but I wouldn't have objected.

I soon established that the dogs weren't allowed in the hotel, so I'd have to sneak them in (hey, they advertised the place as dog friendly – they lied to me, I lied to them. They didn't charge my credit card for extra cleaning so I'm assuming I got away with it). I ordered my dinner and tried to watch a bit of TV to wind down, which is hard to do when all you can see is white lines and bitumen, even when you close your eyes.

An upside to being pregnant was that there was no more insomnia, so I managed to get a good sleep. The extra person I was carrying around obviously wore me out more than I realised.

The next day I woke as early as I could and took off, this time headed for Alice Springs, where I had accommodation booked. Along the way I went to Devils Marbles, a park that I hadn't visited the first time around, because I'd been on my own and the idea had made me nervous. This time, though, a couple of Australian Army trucks had gone in ahead of me so I knew that I wasn't completely alone and also figured the Australian Army weren't exactly going to be like Ivan Milat.

Getting to Alice Springs from Tennant Creek meant passing through Wycliffe Well, Australia's UFO hotspot. In fact, the sign at the entrance to the town reads: WELCOME TO WYCLIFFE WELL, UFO CAPITAL OF AUSTRALIA. Yes, this sign is for real. Not long after that there's another sign saying, EARTHLINGS ALSO WELCOME.

The entire Stuart Highway is made up of funky little truck stops like this one. It's what made the trip so fun. I absolutely love all that kitschy hillbilly shit; I must have taken three thousand photos along the way.

The highway being one of the country's longest tourist routes, I also saw crazy random shit on the side of the road. As I drove, I kept passing these desert 'sandpeople' (like snowmen but made out of sand), made by bored tourists on the side of the highway. The sandpeople were often wearing a T-shirt and a cap, and had painted-on faces. I have no idea how this tradition came about but it seems to be the thing to do if you tour the Stuart Highway. I didn't have the time to stop and build one myself, but next time I'll make sure I take a heap of spare clothes and leave my own sand person behind.

By about 4.30 p.m. I made it to Alice Springs. It had been a nice cruisy day because I'd only had to drive just over six hours, so I had taken my time and the dogs were a lot happier with the number of stops I made compared with the day before. Chaos was a seasoned traveller but Maisie was yet to get the hang of a long-distance car trip. Sometimes while I was driving she'd end up sitting on my head, so I'd have to chuck her back onto Chaos, who would just look at me with an expression that said, 'Yeah, great, thanks for that.' Probably because if she wasn't sitting on my head she was sitting on his, or climbing onto the back ledge of the car and launching herself on top of him, kamikaze style.

I'd booked a 'cabin' (more like a shipping container) in a caravan park just out of the town centre. A friend of mine lived on the other side of Alice Springs but she worked out bush in some of the desert communities as a nutritionist at the time and wouldn't be back in town until late that night, so we arranged to have brekkie together the next morning. The dogs and I had Maccas for dinner, and after cranking up the aircon we settled into our digs for the night.

You wouldn't think, after driving all over the countryside, that I'd get lost in a town like Alice Springs, but I seem to be able to achieve anything once I put my mind to it. It took me about an hour to find my friend's house the next day, so I didn't get to spend as much time with her as I wanted. Since I'd last seen her she'd had two kids. It was pretty surreal – the last time we'd hung out, in Albury, we used to spend our time at the local pub. We had some pretty wild nights back in our day. Now here I was, seven months pregnant, visiting her in the middle of the desert at the large country-style house she shared with her kids. I pulled into the driveway after an hour of driving around in circles and she was out the front with two of the most adorable kids I've seen. My friend introduced me to them.

'This is Kellie, my old friend from school.'

They thought that was amazing. 'You went to school?'

'Yep, back in the olden days your mum and I went to school together,' I told them. I figured I'd save the other stories of what we got up to for when they're older.

I remember being a kid and thinking my parents were born as adults. You don't realise they had a whole other life before you came along. My mate hadn't changed much, although she was probably more settled than when I last saw her. Of course, she was a nineteen-year-old uni student back then! She made me banana pancakes and a cup of tea while we tried to squeeze about eight years' worth of gossip into one hour. Over the past few years she'd been a working single mum. It wasn't easy, she told me, but she seemed to be doing a great job. I wondered how I would cope in the same situation. Although I was starting to suspect that being a 'work widow' was very similar in some ways to being a single parent. I was grateful Dave worked his arse off, meaning that I could take time off for my pregnancy and caring for the baby. I just wasn't sure how I was going to cope without him being there every day to help.

After a breakfast that was much better for me than the Maccas brekkie I usually have when I'm on the road, my friend had to take her kids to kindy and I had to get going so I would reach my next destination by sunset. It was a shame I couldn't stay longer. I had no idea when I'd see her next, but

I had already paid deposits on all of my accommodation for the trip so I had to stick to the schedule.

I stopped for petrol about ninety kilometres south of Alice, in a little place called Stuarts Well. Like most towns along the Stuart Highway, it was tiny, with a big truck stop/caravan park and not much else. I parked out the front and left the dogs outside while I paid for the petrol. The lady who served me asked me about my car and all the stickers. I told her I was doing the Triple J Road Trip Relay and asked if I could take some pictures and get a bit of an interview with her.

'Oh, love, you don't want to talk to me, you want to talk to John, the owner. He's been here for more than twenty years,' she said. As if on cue, a big man with a grey beard, about sixty years old, appeared from some back room and came up to the counter next to his employee.

'Hang around for fifteen minutes. When the tourist bus gets here, Dinky will put on a show for you,' he told me.

Who the fuck was Dinky?

'You got dogs in the car?' John said. 'Cos you don't want 'em anywhere near Dinky, he's getting cranky in his old age.' By this stage I was guessing Dinky was either a cranky old man or a dog. I was half right. John led me to a large dining area featuring an old piano and an ancient-looking dingo lying next to it.

'Meet Dinky, the singing dingo.' When I went to pat Dinky, John quickly stopped me.

'You don't wanna do that,' he warned. 'Dinky can come up to you and if he's comfortable he'll touch you, but you can't touch him or he might bite.' Right. So Dinky was kind of like a stripper, then. Did I have to tip him as well?

I hung around for the next fifteen minutes, and when the tourists came, Dinky put on his show as promised. Not only can this dingo sing, he also plays the piano, the talented bastard. I took some video footage and a million pictures. Dinky is retired nowadays, but you can find old footage on YouTube if you google him.

I was heading to Coober Pedy, SA, a town famous for its underground housing and the opal mines which surround the town. I had booked my accommodation at an underground hotel. And when they say underground they're not kidding! It was just past the Coober Pedy turnoff, down a dirt road full of opal mines. It was kind of like being in a horror movie – a pregnant woman, alone in the desert, staying by herself in an underground cave. Because of all the travel I do alone, I've never been able to sit through the movie *Wolf Creek*.

I drove up a bit further, past all the holes in the desert, and there was a big hill and a driveway, which I assumed was the hotel. Even the office was a cave. The guy gave me a voucher and a menu for a fast-food joint back in town, so I took my stuff to my room then drove back in for a feed. It was outside the takeaway shop on the main street of Coober Pedy that I met Nipper Crab. He was looking at my car, which was still covered in Queen of the Desert stickers but now had a shitload of red dirt all over it as well, in true Territory style.

'Hey, mate, how ya goin'?' I said as I approached him.

'Oh, g'day, I was just checkin' out ya car – it's yours, isn't it?'

'Yeah, mate, I just put the stickers on it to kind of promote this Road Trip Relay thingy I've entered. And, you know, I *am* the Queen of the Desert,' I joked.

'You won't believe this but I was in that movie,' he said. 'You know when the bus got towed? That was me! And I kind of did some work on the set.'

'That's bloody awesome – I should do a story on you for the competition. Do you have a Facebook page or something?'

He wrote his email and Facebook details on the back of a menu I had in the car. 'Stay in touch – I'll also add you to my Facebook group!'

'No worries, mate.' I looked down at the paper. 'Nipper Crab? That's your name?'

'Yeah, mate, long story.' He winked at me. The people he was with started to motion to the restaurant next to the takeaway shop as if to say 'hurry the fuck up and get in here would ya', so I said goodbye and took off back to my cave. I was disappointed I didn't get a chance to do an interview with him for the Road Trip Relay but he was gone before I had the chance. I did end up staying in touch with Nipper, though, keeping up with all the Coober Pedy news on his Facebook group, which is like a social hub for Coober Pedy locals. It might not look like much happens out there, but after reading about some of the shit these boys have done over the years, I know better now.

The night in the underground hotel was a bit scary because apart from the lights in the room, it was pitch black. The toilets were outside and I had to walk at least a hundred metres to get to them. Being pregnant, this was a bit of a pain in the arse and needless to say, I didn't get much sleep. At 6 a.m. I was over it and just wanted to get back on the road, but I thought I'd better get some photos of the underground campsite that was next to the hotel-style rooms in this cave. A tent had been set up with chairs and camp gear outside it the night before, and I'd assumed it was a display tent because I didn't think anyone else was staying there. So I took a few photos, with the flash on of course because it was so bloody dark, when I heard a few coughs then a loud 'ahem'. Oh, fuck. So it wasn't a display tent, then ... I quickly packed up and left before they got up.

Coober Pedy was a bit like being on another planet – the hills seemed to have eyes. I had the creepy feeling that anything could happen there and I'd be lucky to get out alive. There were so many holes in the desert that it was like a set of a horror film. There's some lovely people from there, so I don't want to make out like it's horrible – because it's not. And I never had anything bad happen. It just had that vibe of 'you don't want to stuff up here because there's a lot of places to hide your body'.

Once I left there, I was on my second last day and headed for Broken Hill, another town made famous by the *Priscilla* movie. I had to go through Port Augusta then switch highways as soon as I was on the other side of town.

At Port Augusta, I decided to get something to eat and let the dogs out for a bit of a run around. I parked the car near a big reserve, where I let the dogs go and do their thing before giving them some water and tying them up near the car. Walking to the nearest cafe, I realised that the warm desert air was behind me and I would need to stock up on some ugg boots and trackie pants before I could continue with the rest of my journey.

After raiding the local Big W, I fired up the engine of my Suzuki Swift and took off. It took me four hours to get to Broken Hill from Port Augusta, driving on narrow little country roads. The scenery was changing from the desert to country farms, with the trees getting thicker and the hills greener the further east I drove. I got to Broken Hill, one of the oldest towns in New South Wales, and after finding the caravan park I was booked into, I drove through the town in search of food. As I drove I kept an eye out for the pub that featured in *Priscilla*, but if I saw it, I didn't recognise it. I bought myself some Singapore noodles then went straight to bed, getting up early the next day to complete the last ten hours of my journey. As much as I love a good road trip, by this point I just wanted to get it over with.

I rolled into Albury on 17 November. The outside of my car was covered in red dust, while the inside gave away my on-the-road diet – which had consisted solely of McDonald's for the last forty-eight hours of the trip – and also contained two very patient pit bulls. Mum couldn't believe it.

'You've done a really good job, Kel, I'm so proud of you,' she told me, 'even if you are crazy.'

I was pretty proud of me too. I never did win the Road Trip Relay but I sure had fun completing it. I didn't need to win the comp to know I was Queen of the Desert.

CHAPTER 17

DAVE GOES AWOL

I STAYED DOWN SOUTH FOR SIX WEEKS. I SPENT the first few nights with my mum and Brendon at their Burrumbuttock property. After a week of hanging out with the sheep while they both worked I started to get a bit lonely. This is how I ended up spending most of my time at my old boss's house.

Tinky is about sixty years old and a self-confessed 'plumber from hell'. I used to be his labourer when I was twenty-one. Working with him was a unique experience. I got to learn a whole new language, one that wasn't available as an elective at high school. I also nearly had to go to rehab at the end of my time with him, because back then, before he saw the light, every day at 3 p.m. was 'beer o'clock'. I was whole-heartedly encouraged to join him in this tradition. I can't say I complained, especially as Friday was 'pub lunch day', which meant we rarely went back to work after we stopped for a meal at 12 p.m.

The times we did go back to the job site for the afternoon were pretty hilarious. One afternoon we were working on a bathroom renovation at a house that belonged to a mate of Tinky's, so we didn't even have to wait till lunchtime to get stuck into the VB. Tinky had just installed the new toilet and I asked him if it was okay to use. I swear he said it was ready to use but he reckons I heard wrong – whatever the case, as I was sitting on the loo doing my thing I heard Tinky yelling and cursing from under the house.

'What's the matter, Tink?' I called out, wondering if he'd had a stroke or something.

'Ya fuckin' bloody pissed on me, ya bitch!'

Oops. Apparently the toilet wasn't quite ready after all and Tinky just happened to be finishing off the pipe work under it. Of course, he didn't have to go to the pub and tell the whole bar what had happened. I had to explain to people that I didn't do it on purpose, because the way he told the story you'd think that was the case.

A few years ago, Tinky finally got his driver's licence back after twenty years of driving the gauntlet without it and moved to a small patch of land on the outskirts of town. Deciding that he wanted to hang on to his licence this time, he gave up his daily trip to the pub, and now you'll find him out in his vegie garden, drinking a mid-strength stubby and tending to his plants. He still has all his mates with the weird names coming round for a beer, though. When I used to go to the pub with him years ago, no one had a real name. And half of them were named after some kind of fruit or vegetable – like old Radish (who, unfortunately for him, was the spitting image of one).

Every time I tell Tinky I've travelled somewhere, he asks if I've met some old bloke he knows who lives in the area. When he found out I was living up in the Territory he was like, 'Oh yeah, do you know me mate Cowboy? He's up in Katherine.'

'Well, no, Tinky, I can't say I've seen him, but then Katherine is three hundred kilometres away.'

Tinky would just nod and say, 'Well, when you're in Katherine you should catch up with him. He drinks at one of the pubs in town.'

Old Tink looked after me until Christmas-time, when he made his annual trip up north to see his daughter and grandkids. He always stays with his ex-wife, who ends up getting the shits because Tinky and her new husband usually get on the piss and go fishing for three days without her. Only Tinky would be stoked about his ex remarrying – he just saw it as a new mate he could do bloke stuff with when he was up north.

After Tinky went up to Queensland to spend quality time with his family (his version of it, anyway), I had to drive the four hours to Melbourne with the dogs. I was supposed to be staying at my nan's place for two weeks over Christmas. My nan also had my dad's brother staying there and although he loves dogs, Chaos and Mayhem were driving everyone nuts. I had to keep them chained up most of the time because they took off to the park across the road if I let them roam free. At the time, Victoria was cracking down on dogs that look like mine due to recent attacks by 'pit bulls'. If Chaos and Maisie had been seized they would have been put down, no questions asked. Although it kept them safe, the whinging that came with them being chained up was giving everyone (including me) a headache. To give my uncle and nan a break, I headed down to my dad's house, a further one and a half hours south in a town called Traralgon. It wasn't far from Rosedale, where I'd lived before Mum and Dad divorced. I hadn't been back to the area in years. Driving down the Princes Highway, I started recognising old landmarks, like Gumbuya Park, an animal sanctuary and funpark that we always nagged Mum and Dad to take us to but only went to once because its prices were kind of insane.

When I arrived at Dad's, he was out the back, building the latest extension to his house. My whole life, Dad has been renovating houses. I don't think he will ever be able to live in a house without wanting to knock half of it down and rebuild.

I managed to get him away from his toolbox for a little while, though, and we went to the local shopping centre, which had not changed a bit in the sixteen years I'd been away. We had lunch then headed to Coles to get some groceries when Dad spotted a guy selling remote-control toy aeroplanes.

'Hey, Kel, you should get me one of these for Christmas!' It was as if he was about twelve years old. I guess growing up with five siblings, he probably didn't have a remote-control car when he was a kid. In those days, the way my nan tells it, you were lucky to have shoes on your feet.

When he wandered off to look at some other shiny thing that caught his eye, I rang my brother. He works in the mines in WA and has more money than the rest of our family. He agreed to put half the money in my account, so I bought the plane and gave it to Dad the minute he came back. It would have been a bit hard to sneak into the car without him noticing. He was stoked.

'Hey, Dad, I had an idea – you could tape a camera to it and fly it around the neighbourhood. Think of all the hot chicks you could find!'

'Kel, first of all I live in Traralgon – it's not exactly the Gold Coast. And second, Connie would kill me.'

Connie was Dad's fiancée. After ten years of living it up on oil rigs in Africa, he'd finally settled down with a lady he knew from Rosedale. It was weird seeing Dad in a relationship again, but he seemed happy.

'I was only joking, Dad. If you really pulled a stunt like that, you'd probably get arrested.'

I spent a couple of nights at Dad's, then drove back up to Melbourne where I was meeting the rest of my family for Christmas.

Dave was supposed to fly down from Darwin so we could be together on Christmas Day, but first he had to drive back into town from whichever remote bush community he was currently working at (I'm pretty sure he was in Gapuwiyak but I could never keep track) and catch the plane across to Darwin. It was starting to look a bit harder than it should have been due to an unusual amount of rain that month. Generally East Arnhem Land doesn't flood until January, but this year the rain had come early. Dave had to drive through some rough conditions to get back into Gove.

When I got a phone call from Ben (Dave's workmate who helped us move into our Darwin River house) at 6 a.m. a couple of days before Christmas telling me Dave was stuck out there and his phone was off, my heart sank. In a total panic, Ben had called the bush police and sent them out looking for Dave. Now he told me he was going to drive out there and look for him. In his Toyota Camry. He was already halfway to Katherine.

'Mate, you can't drive out there, you're in a bloody Camry. How the fuck do you think you're going to drive through the bush in that?'

'I dunno what else to do, Kel, I gotta find him. I can't get him on the phone, I've tried the cops – no one's seen him.'

'He's probably broken down, knowing that bloody Cruiser ute. Just go back to Palmerston – there's no use you going out there and getting yourself stuck as well. I'll message a few people on Facebook and try to call his boss – he'll be right, don't worry.' I couldn't believe that here I was, seven and a half months pregnant, trying to calm this bloke down when it was the father of my child who was missing. But Ben sounded like he was about to lose his shit so someone had to think rationally. I didn't really think Dave would be in any trouble; the bloke was pretty handy in a crisis. And if he was stuck, he was forever pointing out berries and crap in the bush that you could eat for survival. Paul Hogan wasn't wrong when he said you can live on it – but it tastes like shit! Dave's vast knowledge of bush survival coupled with his hunting and fishing skills made me pretty confident that we had nothing to worry about.

Sure enough, about six o'clock that night, Dave called me up. 'Bloody Ben, the dickhead, ringing the cops – I tried to tell him I was losing reception out there. I dunno why he panicked – I'd just finished telling him the fuel pump on the Cruiser was fucked and I was gonna be an extra day getting home.'

Dave couldn't understand what all the fuss was about. Apparently he'd called Ben when he knew he wasn't going to get to Gove Airport in time to make his flight into Darwin. He had to stop and manually pump the fuel every hundred kilometres. Finally he made it into Gove but his original plan to fly down to Melbourne and spend Christmas with me was out the window. I was upset he couldn't make it but relieved he'd got back safely to Darwin. I couldn't do much about the situation so I just tried to enjoy my Christmas Day. Everyone was disappointed Dave couldn't be there, especially as he had promised to fly down with mud crabs and barra fillets. But they all understood the crisis and tried to cheer me up.

As well as Dave missing the Christmas celebrations down south, there was the small problem of how to get the Suzuki back to Darwin. I had intended to fly up while Dave drove the car and the dogs back up north, on the condition that I got rid of the Queen of the Desert stickers before he got in the car. No bloody way was I doing that trip again – simply sitting on the couch was starting to get uncomfortable, let alone squeezing into a tiny little car with two dogs, all the luggage and Dave, who's too big for the car anyway. It looked like no one would be going back to Darwin in the Swift now, so I got Mum to drive it back to Albury, where it's still parked in her garage to this day. Brendon followed her in the car they'd driven down in and I booked the dogs on the plane with me, luckily this time getting them on the same flight.

CHAPTER 18

A GOVE DETOUR

IT WAS A RELIEF TO GET BACK UP TO DARWIN after all the travelling I'd done over the past six weeks, and I planned to spend the last few weeks of my pregnancy relaxing. Dave and I had a couple of weeks together before he headed off out bush again. He still hadn't found work in Darwin and I was beginning to suspect he wasn't really in a hurry to leave Gove. I didn't want to pressure him about it, given that I wasn't working myself at that stage.

We spent most of the time lying around the lounge room in the airconditioning as the humidity outside was unbearable. We went to Target and bought a swimming pool, which was about a metre deep. Within half an hour of filling it, the water was like a hot bath. It was nice at night-time, though. Until the mozzies started to attack.

Although I didn't want him to leave, eventually Dave had to go back to work. The further along I was with my pregnancy, the more I hated being left alone. I was trying really hard not to dwell on the fact that I was lonely as hell and set about filling my days with things to keep me occupied. I had already decked out the house with baby stuff. In typical Dave fashion, he'd taken me to a baby supply store and told me to get everything we needed. And I mean everything – we got items from a cot and stroller right down to toys, clothes and three months' worth of nappies. Apart from the odd check-up at the hospital, there was nothing left to do. So I was at a bit of a loose end. Dave suggested I mow the lawns, since I had nothing to do. This isn't as horrible as it sounds. We had a ride-on lawnmower, so in theory it should have been easy. Plus it's snake country out there. You don't want your lawns too long or you won't spot the snakes.

I was going great until I ran over a bit of rope, which wrapped itself around the blade. I did try to get it off but I couldn't do it without turning the lawnmower upside down. I flipped the thing on its side and still couldn't get it, even with a knife. Mum called halfway through this and I copped a lecture about operating heavy machinery while eight months pregnant. I tried to explain that it was a lawnmower, not a tractor, but it wasn't any use. I gave up trying to repair the ride-on mower and finished the job with the regular lawnmower. Well, most of the job, anyway. It broke down just before I could finish but by that stage I was over mowing lawns. I'd have had more luck cutting the grass with a pair of scissors.

To keep fit, I had been going for walks around the park at Berry Springs, but it was getting a bit wet around the area and my croc paranoia was setting in. One afternoon when I went for a walk, the creek started spilling over as I got further along the path and I was forced to walk through water. I don't know if I was being silly but the hairs on the back of my neck stood up and I started waddling as fast as I could back to the car park. I felt like a dickhead at the time, but a couple of weeks later I heard that a large salty was pulled from the creek, so maybe my intuition is better than I thought. After that I decided it was much safer to exercise in numbers, so I took up aquarobics at the local pool. I was the youngest in the class by about thirty years, and before I knew it, I had all the well-meaning oldies lining up to hand out advice. One woman in her sixties started giving me the old 'natural births are best' speech, but the lady beside her soon put a stop to it.

'What a load of bullshit,' she said. 'You can do it without drugs, but I'm telling you, if they'd had all that pain relief available back in my day I would have taken the lot!'

I was with her. I was planning on an epidural, backed up with gas and whatever else was on offer. I didn't want to feel a thing and I wasn't taking any chances.

The local paper was also a great way to fill in the day. They ran stories on everything from crocs appearing in people's swimming pools to UFOs being spotted on the Stuart Highway. Almost every day I would find a newspaper article that made me laugh. The best one, hands down, was the front-page headline 'WHY I STUCK A CRACKER UP MY CLACKER'.

This gem made world news. A 22-year-old Darwin bloke had shoved a firecracker up his own arse and lit the fuse. I'd heard of the 'dance of the flaming arseholes' (where drunk blokes shove toilet paper in their bum cheeks, light it up then dance around trying to get away from it), but this was taking it to a whole new level!

Another pearler was the guy who got knocked out by a flying dildo. The story goes, it was a bucks' night and they hired a stripper to do the type of show I used to sell on the Gold Coast. These shows involve sex toys and, to be honest, I'm surprised guys don't get knocked out by them more often, considering the way they try to get as close as they can to the action. Anyway, this was another story that went viral and became national if not world news. And let's not forget my mate Nicole making the front page for being sacked from a topless bar. The *NT News* is by far the most entertaining newspaper in the country. I couldn't get enough of the crazy stuff they came up with. I ended up collecting the best stories and pictures and making a huge collage, which helped fill in the hours.

Art and craft wasn't something I was fabulous at but I enjoyed it and it filled the time. I even came first in the Palmerston Library art competition – but there were only three of us who entered. Still, Dave reckoned it was awesome that I came first place in a 'capital city'.

At the end of January I spent my thirtieth birthday with Dave in Gove. While he was working, Dave stayed in a little seaside shack in Yirrkala, a small community fourteen kilometres from Gove. Dave and I pretty much lived at the beach, it was so hot and humid. Despite the water being crystal clear, we had to sit back to back in the water so we could spot any approaching crocs. Also the sea lice attacked me one arvo and made me so itchy that I nearly invented a new dance to rival the one of the 'flaming arseholes'.

When I went for a swim all of the local Aboriginal kids hung out with me. Dave reckoned they had probably never seen a pregnant woman in a bikini before (the women in the community don't wear them), so I would have been a bit of a novelty. They are the cutest kids, so friendly and trusting with their big brown eyes and even bigger smiles. Once they decided they liked me they didn't leave my side for the day.

I had them climbing up on my lap, back and head. They used Dave as a diving platform, begging him to dunk them in the water. Once he had done it for one of the kids, that was it. He was stuck playing King of the Kids for about two hours until we managed to sneak away back to our little shack.

I went to the Walkabout pub to see if any of my old mates were there. I was so disappointed when I went back into the Animal Bar. Some city-bred wanker had taken over the place and renovated the whole bar. There was nobody I recognised – in fact, there was barely anybody drinking there at all. It now looked like some soulless TAB bar you would find in the city. All of the character and history of the place had been destroyed. It was one of the saddest things I've seen. Nearly as sad as the time some dentist from Sydney burnt down the heritage-listed Termo hotel in Albury because he'd bought the lease and was going broke. They built a liquor superstore in its place. I just think some things should never change and country pubs are one of them. If you want a fancy club, build one up the road!

Apart from the pub being a bit of a let-down, I had a great time in Gove. Dave is definitely at his happiest out there and it felt like when we had first met, before our lifestyle differences and the distance between us began to take their toll. We hadn't had so much fun together in ages. Usually, when Dave had his time off in Darwin we would argue over stupid stuff like the fact that he thinks it's normal to have to turn on a water pump and wait ten minutes for the water to get to the kitchen tap, then wait another ten minutes for the water to turn from brown to clear. I would reply, 'Yeah, if you lived in 1922, I'm sure this would have been the height of luxury. It's 2013, Dave, most people have modern plumbing in their homes these days!' Our lifestyle differences were pretty obvious when he came back to town. Dave's not the sort of person who thinks living in a glorified shed in the middle of nowhere is roughing it. He kind of expected me to deal with all the shit that comes with bush living while he was away. I'm a lot of things but I'm not a mechanic, or a washing-machine repair person or a bloody lawnmower doctor. But Dave can do all of these things and expects everyone else to be capable of them as well. Meanwhile, if I had wanted to stick my bloody head under a bonnet all day, I'd have done a mechanic apprenticeship!

Since I'd been in Gove, though, we hadn't had one argument. It crossed my mind that our relationship might not be so volatile if I lived back out there. But after my last experience of living in Gove, I knew that in reality I'd be miserable after a month.

On the morning of my birthday we were up at six. Actually, both of us had been lying awake since midnight due to a power cut to the Yirrkala community. Without electricity the airconditioner was useless and we'd had no option but to open all the doors and windows of his tiny shack, inviting the mozzies to come and join us for the night. So by 6 a.m. we had given up trying to sleep and headed into town for brekkie. We grabbed a takeaway coffee and bacon and egg roll each and headed to Middle Beach, just past the Gove golf course, where we caught the last of the sunrise. The perfect end to a shitty night.

When we got back to the shack, I had a nap and woke up to a lounge room full of balloons and presents. While I was asleep, Dave had snuck into town and raided the only gift shop in Gove. Later that night we went out for dinner with a couple of friends. Afterwards he gave me the best present I could have received. No, not any bedroom shenanigans – though that came later!

The best present I got all day was Dave's blessing for the name I had chosen for our little Gumnut baby. It had been another thing we couldn't seem to agree on. Although Dave generally couldn't care less about other people's opinion of him, he was still pretty old school and thought the name I had chosen would make people think we were pot-smoking hippies. I pointed out that they wouldn't be far off the mark and he just told me not to be a bloody smart-arse. But it seemed that Dave had finally come around and accepted the name I had chosen. I'd secretly hoped he would. It was a bit like the time I made him a roast pumpkin and spinach pasta dish. He sat at the table and stared at it for ten minutes, looking at the pasta then looking at me, wondering where the meat was and why I was forcing him to eat weird vegetarian food. But after he tried it, he loved it. So I knew it was only a matter of time before he got used to the name I had picked: Marli Rose.

A week later I had to leave because Dave was due to fly back out bush and after my Ramingining experience I knew I wouldn't be very comfortable if I joined him. I just hoped he'd be coming back to Darwin soon. I was anxious about the whole giving-birth thing and didn't want there to be any chance of him getting stuck out bush when it happened.

'When do you think you're going to be in Darwin? It's nearly time for me to have the baby. I don't want to be on my own when I go into labour.'

'I told you, I'll be there the week before, I promise.'

'We still haven't sorted out your living arrangements, though. I thought you would be living there by now.' I didn't want to fight with him after we'd had such a good time, but I couldn't help bringing it up.

'Kel, I told ya, I'm doing everything I can. You see how much stuff I've got over here, it's going to take a while before I can get it all out.'

I'd heard that before. There wasn't any point fighting about it, though. He'd given me an awesome birthday and I knew he was doing his best. I also knew, especially now, that he didn't really want to leave Gove at all.

CHAPTER 19

THE WORLD'S WORST UTE

OUR CAR SITUATION FINALLY CAME TO A head when I was thirty-seven weeks pregnant. I went for a routine check-up at the hospital but before I got there two of the tyres on the ute blew. The first time, I was halfway to Palmerston when I heard a huge bang and nearly jumped through the windscreen, thinking there'd been a gunshot or something. I pulled over to the side of the road, hopped out of the car and looked at the front wheels. The front driver's side tyre had blown. It was shredded to pieces. I had no idea what to do because, being a proper four-wheel-drive tyre, it was about as tall as my shoulders. Luckily, I had a spare one in the back of the ute, and a bloke passing by took pity on me and changed the tyre. Half an hour later, as I was driving through town, almost at the hospital, the back driver's side tyre blew out. By this time I was completely fucked; the day was boiling hot and there was no way I'd be able to fix anything with my huge pregnant belly. I kind of collapsed in defeat on the side of the road and called Terri, my mate from the pub, who seemed to be my hero whenever one of those bloody Cruisers decided to have a shit fit.

She met me there as soon as she could. I didn't have another tyre in the ute tray so we had to take her car all the way back to Darwin River and get the spare ones Dave had stored in the shed. I tried to help her lug them to her car and she nearly killed me.

'For fuck's sake, Kel, leave the bloody thing!' She took the tyre I was trying to roll across the lawn off me before I fell over.

'Sorry, I just feel bad that you have to lift everything.'

'Don't feel bad, mate, I'm just pissed off that the car keeps fucking up on ya and you're stuck out here – it's bullshit!'

'Yeah, I know, but the Suzuki is in Albury and the troopy doesn't even have brakes so this is kinda my only option at the moment.'

'Yeah, well, this option sucks.'

I laughed. 'You're not fuckin' wrong, mate!'

After Terri had thrown two spare tyres in the back of her car, we headed back to the site of what I had now christened 'The Biggest Piece of Shit on Earth' and stood on the side of the road, trying to get the attention of some handy man to come and change the tyre for us. No one pulled over, and I told Terri it was because I was preggers. If we had been two hot chicks trying to get help we would have had twenty cars pull over, but in my huge, blimped-out state, I looked more like a pissed-off tomato than a damsel in distress. In the end I stood on the other side of the ute, and Terri, who is blonde and pretty with a great bod on her, managed to get a bloke to stop and change the tyre for us.

'Right,' she said, once the second tyre had been fixed. 'You need to get on Dave's case about a new car now. What if you go into labour and this happens, Kel? It's bullshit – you can't rely on this piece of crap.'

'Shhh, it'll hear you and bust another tyre if you're not careful,' I joked. 'Yeah, I know, I need to do something about the car situation – I swear Dave just leaves it like this because he thinks it will make life interesting while he's not home!'

Terri laughed. 'Yeah, well, if that's the case I'd rather be fuckin' bored. Will you be right to get into town now?' she asked as she got into her car.

'Yeah, mate, surely it can't blow another tyre – I reckon I've driven over something sharp on my driver's side and it's popped both wheels.'

'I'd say so,' Terri agreed. 'All right, well, just call me if you need to, I'll be home all day.'

'No worries, cheers, mate – you're the bomb diggity!'

She laughed at me and drove off, and I got back in the ute and did the same.

When I finally made it to my hospital appointment, they decided to do a scan because the baby was in a weird position and they wanted to make sure everything was normal. The guy who normally did the ultrasound was training a doctor that day and she took my scan instead. For some reason, against the advice of the qualified expert who was instructing her, she decided something was wrong with the blood flow in the umbilical cord and told me I would have to stay in the hospital overnight. The next day they would most likely have to induce me if the reading was the same. As you can imagine, I was pretty upset and a bit scared for my baby. They even mentioned an emergency caesarean. I called Dave and told him he'd better fly home. As soon as I did that, they told me I could go home and get my hospital bag, as I'd most likely have the baby in the next two days. So I got into The Biggest Piece of Shit on Earth and drove back out to Darwin River. I was nearly home when the car started to lose power. It slowed down from a hundred kilometres an hour to about two kilometres an hour.

'For fuck's sake!' I pulled the piece of junk over to the side of the road, jumped out, popped the bonnet, slammed the door and kicked the bullbar. 'Why are you doing this to me?'

I cried to the car, completely exhausted and miserable after the day I'd had. By now I was feeling well and truly sorry for myself. But before I let my little pity party go too far, I remembered my unborn child and the fact that I needed to get back to the hospital. I dried my eyes and climbed up on the bullbar so I could reach the button that pumped the fuel back down the line and get the ute going again. I had to do that about every three kilometres until I got home, where, because Terri had been called into work, I had to ring Dave's idiot mate Steve.

I couldn't stand Steve, who was having a very open affair with an Irish backpacker as part of a midlife crisis. His poor wife was about to give birth as well, and I really didn't want to sit in a car with the douchebag for an hour. But everyone else I knew in Darwin would be working or drinking at a pub somewhere, and Dave's other mate Ben was in Gove with him. So I was left with no choice. I called Steve and asked him to drive me to the hospital. He came and got me about half an hour later and I braced myself for what would no doubt be an awkward conversation. I did appreciate that he was helping me, and I probably could have got over the whole backpacker thing, but then he spent the entire trip to the hospital explaining to me why it was his wife's fault that he'd decided to go out and root a 21-year-old backpacker on the side. I asked him if he'd ever thought about relocating to the Gold Coast because it sounded like he'd fit right in. I don't think he realised that I was being a smart-arse, because he told me no, but he'd give it some thought.

As much of a tool as this guy could be, he meant well in his own weird way, and after dropping me off at the hospital, he told me he would pick up Dave and bring him there to see me as soon as he got into town.

I went into the hospital and asked the admin lady where I was supposed to go.

'You're staying in the maternity ward,' she said.

'What? Why are they putting me there? I'm still pregnant,' I said. 'Surely I could go to a quieter ward until I have my own screaming newborn to deal with?'

She raised an eyebrow. 'You're about to have a baby; you'll have to get used to the crying at some point.'

After a few deep breaths, the urge to knock her lights out passed. I didn't even want to be there and now I had to try to get some rest in the noisiest section of the hospital? I was scared for my baby, upset and completely alone, and this nurse was treating me like I was a bitch for wanting to get a few hours' sleep without a baby screaming in the bed next to me. Would they make someone who had broken their leg stay in the maternity ward? I couldn't see why I had to stay there when I clearly hadn't given birth yet. I tried to explain this nicely to the nurse but I probably didn't come across as politely as I wanted to.

'Yeah, but I haven't actually had it yet, have I? Doesn't that mean I belong in a different ward – like, I dunno, antenatal or something? I mean, c'mon, it could be my last baby-free sleep on earth and you want to put me in a room with a bunch of newborns?'

'I'm sorry, but that's the only place we have for you,' she said, looking at me like I was the most ungrateful person she'd ever dealt with. As if she would prefer to sleep in a room full of screaming babies instead of her own comfy bedroom at home.

'Fine,' I said, following her to the maternity ward.

'Here, this room is the furthest from the babies. Hopefully you won't be disturbed too much,' she said pointedly.

'No worries, thanks so much.' I looked at the doorway, which seemed to be missing a door. This was going to be a great night, I could tell already.

I tried to get as much sleep as I could, which wasn't much at all, really, so I was up and at 'em by 6 a.m. the next day.

Dave flew into town that morning and came straight to the hospital, where they told us both that we would have to wait until late that afternoon before a decision could be made about my situation. Dave was ready to kill them by this stage, so I thought we'd better get out of the hospital for a while. We went and had breakfast at a cafe in the local shopping centre.

Finally, at about 4 p.m. they took me down for another scan where they informed me that, yes, the qualified guy was right yesterday, my baby was fine and I could go home now. What the hell was going on? Why didn't they just listen to him in the first place instead of the doctor-in-training?

To Dave's disgust, the doctor who gave us this news (without an apology for the stress they had caused us) then tried to tell us that part of the reason I was in hospital was because they were also worried about infections such as parvo. You know, the virus that kills puppies. I sat there wondering if she even was a doctor, or if the hospital was so short-staffed they'd accidentally employed a vet. A simple 'sorry we stuffed up' probably would have been a more appropriate thing to say.

But it was thanks to the doctors stuffing up the scan results that I got a new car. I think Dave felt so sorry that I'd had to deal with so many fuckwits in twenty-four hours that he bought me a Holden Commodore station wagon that had air-fucking-conditioning! Woohoo, praise the lord, I could finally drive in comfort! It even had a bullbar, so while I was driving my new 'limo' I still had a bit of protection from the roos that love to play chicken with the traffic out bush. That bullbar has come in pretty handy a few times when it comes to driving through the city too.

CHAPTER 20

THE ARRIVAL OF THE GUMNUT BABY

'KEL, WHAT THE FUCK ARE YOU DOING?'
I looked up at Dave from the floor. 'The lady at the health clinic told me to massage my boobs – it's supposed to induce your labour.'

'Right, so why are you doing a headstand then?'

'I think it's supposed to help make the baby face the right way.'

'Who told you that shit?'

'I dunno, I think it was on one of those baby blog websites … anyway, it can't hurt.'

'It will if you fall and break ya bloody neck, ya goose! Can't you just lie on the couch like a normal person?' Dave was probably starting to regret coming back in from the bush to keep me company in my final days of pregnancy.

'I just really want the baby to come out now,' I groaned. 'I haven't been able to sleep properly for weeks and I've given up trying to see my feet.'

'Yeah, well, you're not going to get much sleep for the next five years so you may as well get used to it now!' Dave winked at me then quickly got out of there before I could find something to throw at his head. I was not embracing my pregnancy like they do in the books the health nurse gave me. Pictures of beautifully made-up pregnant women drinking cups of herbal tea and practising yoga did not match my particular experience. Why didn't they print pamphlets of bloated women with puffy faces lying on the couch in their boyfriend's oversized Bintang singlet and a pair of granny knickers (well, they *are* bloody comfy!), eating their third bowl of Crunchy Nut Corn Flakes? That'd be a lot closer to the truth.

By the time I hit my due date I'd clocked up some serious telly time. The rain we had experienced in December had disappeared, leaving us with the longest build-up since god knows when. It was that disgustingly hot and humid that you would work up a sweat having a shower. And cop about 347 mozzie bites in the process. Walking from the house to the car required a sweat towel and water bottle – and don't get me started on the outside dunny ... Let's just say that if you had to go to the loo you needed to take with you some insect repellent, a shoe big enough to squash a huntsman spider, five mozzie coils and a portable fan.

Between the mozzies and the humidity, leaving the lounge room was a bit like the TV show *Man vs Wild*, so Dave and I avoided it as much as possible. This explains why we owned the boxed set of every TV show that had aired in the past eighteen months. So we hid out in our little cave made of rocks and cement – very appropriate, because in the last few weeks of my pregnancy a cave woman was exactly what I looked like. Well, I sure as shit felt like one, anyway.

I was due to have the baby on 2 March. The whole day went by and nothing happened, so I went to bed about 9 p.m., although I can't say it was all that comfy. Dave had put a bloody tarp under the fitted sheet in case my waters broke in my sleep. 'Otherwise we'll have to throw the mattress out,' he explained when I asked him what the fuck he was doing. He'd also made me sit on five folded-up towels whenever I got in the car for the past four days.

I woke up at 11 p.m. and needed the loo, where – tada! – my waters broke. I went into shock and suddenly felt sick with anxiety. Shaking, I called the hospital while Dave ran around getting my baby bag, water and god knows what else packed into the car. They told me to come straight in so we drove the seventy kilometres into Darwin. Anxiety easing a bit, I suddenly found I was really hungry, so Dave detoured through Maccas and I got myself a feed that I'd finished by the time we got to the hospital. As soon as we walked through the doors I hit up the vending machine and stuffed myself with chocolate all the way to the maternity ward.

The nurse on duty was about twenty years old, and after talking to her for two minutes it became clear to me that the less she had to deal with, the better. She took me to a room and told me to lie on the bed, which I did, munching away on a Mars Bar while she strapped one of those CTG things on my belly. She left the room, mentioning something about coming back soon. I didn't really give a shit – at this point I was too busy eating chocolate, texting my mum and wondering if this was as painful as it got. At this stage I barely felt a thing and was starting to feel overconfident about the whole giving-birth procedure. If this was the pain they were going on about, it'd be a breeze, I thought to myself.

The nurse came back and, after looking at the machine I was hooked up to, informed me that I wouldn't be going into labour for at least twenty-four hours and in fact they would probably have to induce me. That sounded strange to me, because I thought that since my waters had already broken, my baby was well and truly on its way into the world. But she was supposed to be the expert, not me, so I took the pills she gave me for the 'pain' (I'd be grateful for them soon!) and Dave and I drove back out to Darwin River.

I don't know how the hell I slept, but those pills must have settled my nerves, because one minute I was lying in bed trying to get comfy, and the next thing I knew I was waking up with the most intense period pain I've ever had in my life. Then I remembered it wasn't my period and shit was probably going to get a lot worse from here. I called out to Dave then ran to the loo, where I sat with my head down the toilet for about ten minutes. I hadn't been so sick at 4 a.m. since I gave up indulging in twenty-four-hour benders.

Eventually, I pulled myself off the ground and stumbled into the shower, where I clung to the wall like a drowned rat, doubled over in pain. Okay, so it *did* hurt; obviously I was no longer delusional about that! But then I had this strange urge to push and I realised we were in a whole heap of trouble if I did. The fact that we were living in a bloody shed in the middle of the bush an hour from the hospital was just one of many problems with the situation. (Once Dave had tried to assure me that he would know what to do, after helping countless cows give birth while he was working on a farm. 'Do I look like a fucking cow to you?' was my response at the time and, wisely, he said no of course not and then disappeared to the safety of his toolshed.)

I heard Dave in the kitchen, banging around.

'Dave, are you doing the dishes?' I called out from the shower in disbelief.

'Yep, just let me know when you want to start getting ready to leave.'

'Um, I thought that's what we were doing?' I yelled back, wondering how the hell I was going to get from the shower to the car. 'I'm about to have the baby in the fucking shower!'

'Wait! Don't do that!' I heard a loud crash as he abruptly stopped washing whatever dish he was holding. 'I'll get the car to the door then I'll come get you.'

Five minutes later I was in the car and on my way back to the hospital. Dave kept asking me how my contractions were going and what the timing was or some shit, but all I wanted him to do was stop asking me questions and just drive as fast as he could without getting arrested. I couldn't talk, couldn't listen and couldn't open my eyes. And Dave couldn't believe it. He was sure I'd turn all abusive and violent as soon as I went into labour. But it was like I was hypnotised or something. I just sat as still as I could and hung on to the dashboard, trying really hard not to have the baby on the front seat.

After what felt like five hours we finally made it to the hospital, where I had to stop about three times because of the contractions before we even made it to the front door.

Just as we were about to enter the hospital, some bloke who knew Dave from Arnhem Land came up to him.

'Hey, Dave, I haven't seen you for ages, you got a smoke?' He completely ignored me standing there, about to give birth. If I came close to abusing anyone it was this guy. The look I gave him probably still haunts him to this day.

After stopping a few more times on the way to the maternity ward we eventually made it. This time there was no question of whether or not I was in labour; I was shuttled straight into a room of my own. Leaning up against the bed, I looked up at the nurse. 'Okay, I know I can't have an epidural but can I please have some pethidine now?' I panted between contractions.

The nurse, a woman in her fifties, looked at me with a small amount of sympathy in her eyes. 'Sorry, love, it's too late for all that,' she said. 'You have to get up on that bed and start pushing now. All I can offer you is some gas.' She held out the little gas tube and I grabbed it off her and sucked in a whole heap of the shit. It wasn't very helpful but at least it was some distraction from the pain.

I had two nurses with me by now – the other one was in her twenties (luckily not the same nurse who had sent me away earlier) – and both of them tried to convince me to get up on the bed. After arguing with them for ten minutes,

I finally did what I was told. They kept urging me to push, and I got pissed off then because what did they think I was doing? But it was hard enough trying to breathe, let alone yell at anyone. Then, as I got closer to the finish line, a nurse offered to put a mirror down where the action was so I could watch too.

'No bloody way!' I was horrified at the thought. 'The fact that I have to feel what's going on is bad enough!' Who in their right mind would want to watch that?!

After the most excruciating pain I've ever felt in my life, the older midwife held up a tiny purple baby. I went into shock again. For some reason I remember thinking I didn't recognise her. I don't know why but I thought she would come out looking exactly like Dave, minus the beard. Instead she was the prettiest little thing with rosebud lips and huge blue eyes. They put her in my arms and she didn't cry, she just looked up at me with her big inquisitive eyes and then looked around the room, probably wondering where the hell she was and why it was so bright.

'Welcome to the world, Marli Rose.' I was amazed at how beautiful and calm she was. And those eyes! It was the proudest day of my life. I fell in love with her instantly. They took her off me to give her the injections they give all newborn babies, and when she cried for the first time I nearly lost my shit. So this is what mother love is. I thought my worries would be over once she was born healthy and safe. But I had just realised that this was only the beginning of a lifetime full of worry. After her needles, they weighed her. She was tiny, just under 2.5 kilos. But she was perfectly healthy.

The nurses suggested I feed her, so I did, then I passed her to her father, who by this stage was pretty keen to have his first cuddle with his baby girl – and took 5367 photos.

Because of the bullshit I'd been through with the hospital I decided I wanted to go home that night, knowing I'd be way more comfortable in my queen-size bed with only one screaming baby to wake me every few hours instead of a whole wardful of them. (Although Marli never really did cry much.) So we drove home that night, stopping at Domino's on the way for a large pizza.

Mum called while we were waiting in the car park. 'You just gave birth and now you're in a car park waiting for pizza?'

'Yeah, Mum,' I said. 'Have you forgotten what hospital food tastes like or something?'

Marli Rose spent her first night on earth in a bush hut listening to the tree frogs and crickets as she drifted off to sleep. My little Gumnut baby. I hadn't slept so well in years, obviously worn out by the day's events. Marli must have been equally exhausted, because she slept for seven hours straight. When I woke up the next morning I felt like a kid waking up on Christmas Day. I couldn't remember the last time I'd felt so happy and excited. The happiness I felt was just too amazing to put into words, really. All I knew was that I got to keep her forever and it was the best feeling.

Of course it wasn't all sunshine and lollipops. I knew I'd have to get up a bit during the night; I just didn't realise how long babies took to feed. Then I'd have to burp her and that could take ages. I have no idea how women in the past got through this shit before technology. My iPhone was a godsend at 4 a.m. while I was feeding Marli. I quickly discovered Pinterest and would spend hours pinning pictures of food and craft ideas that I would never, ever use.

For the first couple of weeks, I'd feed her then take her in to Dave, who was camped out on a mattress in the lounge room so he could get some sleep while I fed the baby. He would then wake up and burp her for me so I could sneak in a bit of sleep myself. Otherwise, by the time I finished burping her, she'd just want more food!

We went back to hibernating in the airconditioned lounge room again, only this time I had a baby stuck to my boobs most of the time. If she wasn't feeding, she was on Dave's shoulder or lying in a little bassinet on the floor between us.

Both of us were pretty sleep-deprived, but because Dave had taken time off it was a lot easier than doing it all by myself. We also had a steady stream of family visiting, my mum and sister arriving before Marli was one week old. (Poor Brendon was stuck at home looking after their dogs.) My sister, Naomi, who lives in an inner-city suburb of Melbourne and is a lawyer, has never been crazy about babies, so we were all surprised when she offered to change Marli's nappy. And even more surprised when, after she was covered in baby poo when Marli decided she wasn't quite finished yet, Naomi nearly cried laughing! This was a relief, because for a moment there I didn't think Naomi would touch her again until Marli was toilet-trained. Mum was super-excited about becoming a grandmother for the first time, so I didn't really see my daughter while Mum was up unless Marli needed a feed.

Next up were my dad and brother, who had no clue how to deal with newborn babies and ran from the room in terror if I even mentioned I was about to feed Marli. They coped with the whole situation by making sure they had a steady supply of beer at hand. Actually, I didn't see my brother for about three days. After a day in Darwin River he must have been bored, because next thing I knew, some friend he hadn't seen for ten years came and picked him up, taking him into Mitchell Street, the number one spot to find leggy

Swedish backpackers (and Irish ones, come to think of it). I called Mum to complain and she explained that men don't get as excited about babies as women do. I actually think my brother thought the baby would be born walking and talking. He brought her a T-shirt back from Thailand that was a size five and had 'Gangnam Style' written across it and a picture of that crazy Korean guy who sang it. He also brought back with him a Ninja Turtle tattooed on his bum with the acronym 'YOLO' underneath. I have to admit, I was pretty bloody proud. Most blokes these days go for the tribal sleeve tattoos. There is nothing more hilarious than a skinny little white guy with tribal tatts (what tribe are you from, bro?).

Dad presented me with a gift that was supposed to be from my nan – she'd given him some money to buy it. I opened it up. It was a grey and white jumpsuit that said 'Welcome to Melbourne'. I looked at Dad with raised eyebrows.

'Sorry, I forgot, then I was at the airport and it was too late to go to the normal shops, and this was the only baby thing I could find.'

I just laughed. 'Geez, you're a classic, Dad. At least I know where I get it from.'

I didn't mind them getting on it and having a good time. Having a baby had made me quite relaxed about stuff I would normally get pissed off about. Besides, if I hadn't been breastfeeding I probably would have joined in the party. Apart from the fact that I hadn't had a drink in months, it was great beer-drinking weather. But you don't really need alcohol when you're sleep-deprived. I was hallucinating naturally most days. I wish I'd known about this when I was twenty. I would have saved a lot of money on mind-altering drugs if I had just stayed awake for three days at a time.

Marli spent the first seven weeks of her life in the Territory, in the stormiest part of the year. She had no fear of the thunder or rain; in fact, she loved being outside when a storm was coming. We would walk around the yard and she'd gaze up at the lightning with a serene expression on her face. This didn't surprise me, considering that before she was born, her father and I used to drive out to the back paddock whenever a storm came so we had a clear view of the lightning and the dark clouds rolling in as if they were touching the ground. The storms in the Territory are bloody magical.

Dave and I took her to the Litchfield Park waterfalls, where she had her first 'swim', and for long walks through the bush near the Darwin Dam. She had her first bath under the trees in our front garden. At night-time, her lullaby was a symphony of tree frogs and crickets. She was the original Gumnut kid.

CHAPTER 21

THE EARTHWORM

AFTER A WHILE DAVE HAD TO GO BACK TO work and the reality of our relationship issues returned. Living in a glorified shed with a newborn baby, a million miles from my family and close friends, was taking its toll on me. There were snakes everywhere – including my own kitchen. One night, after I'd fed Marli and put her to bed, I walked out to the kitchen to get a drink and saw a strange-looking piece of rope on the ground between Chaos and Maisie. I thought it might have been a bikini string because it was shiny with black and white stripes. But something stopped me from picking it up. My primal instincts told me to stand on the opposite side of the room and throw things at it instead. Good move, because after I threw a steak knife at its head, the piece of rope came to life and was very, very pissed off.

By this stage Chaos and Maisie had hightailed it outside (possibly more afraid of me than the snake they let into the bloody house in the first place). I freaked out and ran after them, grabbing my mobile on the way, and called Dave, who was about a thousand kilometres away at the time.

'There's a fucking snake in the kitchen! I don't know what to do – it came right at me with its head raised, all pissed off and shit.' I was nearly in tears. I had only just mastered the art of killing huntsman spiders, and even then I needed half a can of Mortein to get the job done.

Dave tried to calm me down. 'It's all right, Kel, just get a broom and push it out the door.'

'A broom?' I said. 'A fucking broom? You want me to sweep the pissed-off snake up with a broom? Are you crazy? What if it bites me? I have no fucking idea what kind of snake it is! How will I get to the hospital? Drive myself? Oh my god, I can't do this! It's a snake, I don't do snakes!'

'Kel, calm down, I can't do anything from here. Can you call Steve up and get him around to help?'

Steve had just moved the Irish backpacker into the family home while his wife was in hospital giving birth to their third child, so I wasn't actually speaking to him. 'I'm not calling that dickhead, I'd rather sleep in the car. Don't worry, I'll call Terri – she might be braver than me.'

As it turned out, Terri had been having a Sunday drinking sesh that afternoon with her boyfriend, and as much as the

Dutch courage probably would have helped her move the snake, there was no way she could drive. Picking her up was out of the question because I couldn't leave the Gumnut or risk the snake disappearing into another part of the house. I had no other option but to call the local pub.

The barmaid was very sympathetic to my situation and promptly sent her boyfriend over to the house to get rid of my intruder. By this stage I had calmed down enough to go back inside, and when I saw the snake, which was now curled up in the corner near the kitchen sink, I was slightly embarrassed. It was the size of a large worm. Okay, maybe a bit bigger, but not much. When the guy from the pub arrived, I sheepishly pointed out the snake and asked him to see if he could move it to the garden, because I didn't want it to die; it looked kind of cute all coiled up in the corner.

Cute. Ha! The snake went absolutely ballistic when the bloke from the pub tried to scoop it up with an empty pizza box. It started thrashing itself around, bouncing along the kitchen floor like it was possessed. 'See!' I exclaimed. 'That's why I was shitting myself before – the bloody thing is mental!'

My hero wasn't looking as confident as when he first walked in, and he ended up dancing around the kitchen, dodging the psychotic snake, every now and then making a half-hearted attempt to get it to jump into the pizza box. Finally, he gave up on getting the snake out alive and smashed it with the pizza box, decapitating my uninvited guest and ending the great 'dance of the snake'. He went to throw it into the garden as I'd originally asked him to do, albeit slightly less alive than I had intended. 'Wait, I gotta get a photo!' I told him, and took a few happy snaps to show Dave when he got home. Which I wish I hadn't done, because to this day if I mention the snake intrusion in front of him he pisses himself laughing and says, 'Snake? Don't you mean earthworm?'

Although Dave found the situation amusing, it brought up fears I hadn't had before. What if something happened to me out there? Who would help me get to hospital? What if I was unconscious and couldn't call for help? What would happen to Marli? Living like a backpacker is all very well and good when it's just yourself you need to worry about. But now I had a tiny little baby living in a place that, let's face it, would probably be condemned if the council ever bothered to visit.

This was when I started to talk to Dave about moving away from the Territory. When he came back to Darwin, we discussed our options.

'Dave, I love the bush but I can't do this any more. I feel so bloody isolated, now more than ever. I've toughed it out living on my own while you've been away for a couple of years now. I've tried so hard to learn to love it but it's killing me not having anyone but you up here.'

Now that I had Marli I was more homesick than ever for the east coast, my family and normal weather. Terri was moving away to Toowoomba, Queensland, and most of my mates in Darwin were under twenty-five and nowhere near having babies. Dave was still absent most of the time. Relationships are hard work anyway, but the obstacles between us were pretty huge.

'Kel, I can't just pack up and leave. I've lived in Gove for ten years now. I need to get my gear out, and the jobs in Darwin are all short contracts. I have a good job in Gove.' He looked as miserable as I felt. He knew I didn't want to move over there. And I knew he didn't want to leave.

In the end, after a couple of months of me trying really hard to convince Dave to come with me, we agreed that I would move away with Marli, and Dave would stay in Gove. He wasn't happy to see us go but he understood that while Gove was where he belonged, it was never going to be my home.

We left on a 9 p.m. flight. Marli was just under three months old and so tiny and vulnerable. The poor dogs, who were coming with me, were stored in cargo. I bet they were sick of planes by this stage – they'd only just flown back from Melbourne to Darwin a few months beforehand.

I boarded the plane with a heavy heart. Regardless of our differences, I loved Dave, and leaving wasn't easy, not one bit. I remembered my excitement when we first got together and the night I flew back into Gove with Chaos and all my gear. I never thought I'd be leaving the Territory without him.

The flight from Darwin to Melbourne is about four and a half hours long. Marli slept the whole time, although I don't know how. Across the aisle, a little girl was crying and screaming for her daddy, who obviously wasn't there. I had to fight my emotions as I listened to her cry. I thought about what I was doing and how it was going to affect our little family. I never wanted to take Marli away from her dad. I just hoped I could make sure they spent as much time together as possible.

Mum and Brendon picked me up from Tullamarine Airport at 1 a.m. Compared with Darwin it seemed huge. Once we got in the car and started travelling up the Hume Highway towards Albury, I finally felt settled enough to close my eyes and fall asleep.

CHAPTER 22

THE QUIET LIFE

AFTER A COUPLE OF MONTHS BUMMING around at my mum's house, and lots of trips up to the New South Wales mid-north coast, I moved to a little town there called Karuah.

Karuah is famous for its oysters and wood-chopping. They even have an annual Oyster and Timber Festival – I'm not making that up. Dave comes down every couple of months and I take Marli to see him when I can. It was weird at first, me moving away and us not seeing each other, but after a few months we settled into our new lifestyle. I still harass Dave at work when I'm bored and want to have a chinwag to someone, so not much has really changed there. He was probably relieved to have a bit of peace and quiet, but unfortunately for him, just because we aren't together any more doesn't mean I don't talk his ears off when he gives me a chance.

I do get 'homesick' for the Northern Territory and am glad I have a good excuse to visit a couple of times a year.

I still supply skimpies for the Airport Tavern and recently went back up to do a few shifts myself and say g'day to the blokes who became mates when I worked there.

Marli is a true-blue Territorian and I want her to grow up with the culture and experiences you only get in the Territory. Dave has a lot of cool shit to show her – I'm certainly not the person to teach her how to gut a fish.

I swore I wouldn't go back to skimpy work after I became a mum, but I missed it too much. Not many other jobs allow you to make so much money in so little time, while having a ball doing it. You can now find me, on any given afternoon, holding the floor at one of the old pubs in the Hunter Valley/Newcastle region, telling crazy bush tales to coal miners while I serve them drinks, dressed in lingerie. Business as usual.

I didn't know anyone when I first moved to Karuah, but in a town this size it's hard to remain anonymous. Especially with Chaos and Maisie escaping to roam the streets every second day. Because Maisie grew up on our fifty-acre Darwin River property, she thinks the entire town is her domain. I usually find them outside the local butcher's, who takes pity on their puppy-dog eyes and throws them a bone or two. So far I've spent $500 in pound fees. Next time I'll bloody leave them there.

I found myself a little house that overlooks the Karuah

River and has a vegie patch and a chook shed out the back. Of course, I don't have any chooks due to Chaos and Maisie, but the vegie patch is going well. I'm a bit scared to actually eat the vegies, though, because I have no idea what those two get up to in the yard while I'm not looking. I'm not real keen on eating vegies that are covered in dog piss.

Karuah is definitely somewhere I can see myself living for a while. The whole Port Stephens area is amazing – a great combination of both the bush and the beach, with the Hunter Valley not far away. That really sealed the deal, because the Hunter region produces two of my favourite things: food and wine. As well as stuffing my face, I'm keen to try sandboarding – the sand dunes around here are like ski slopes. I looked at buying a board but after seeing the price I decided a bit of cardboard would do me just fine. Actually, one of the volunteer ladies from the Karuah information centre suggested I pinch a real estate sign and use that. God, I love the locals here!

I'm happy for the moment, although the gypsy in me is always dreaming up another adventure to embark on. Unlike some girls, my fantasy life doesn't include luxury resorts, limos or day spas. Maybe it used to, way back before I left the Gold Coast in search of adventure. A lot has changed since I moved from the city to the bush.

Living in the Northern Territory for nearly three years with Australia's answer to Bear Grylls sure has changed my outlook on life. I've learnt that nothing is impossible if you want it badly enough. Four years ago I was stuck in a rut, dreaming of a life I was too afraid to live. But once I took that chance I realised I could do whatever I wanted: I could survive living in isolated communities, I could drive across the country solo, I could be a V8 Supercar Grid Girl, I could feature as a model for the local newspaper and I could land myself a daily spot on commercial radio! Never would I have thought any of this was possible four years ago. I'd finally learnt that all I had to do was grab life by the balls and truly live it.

These days, my fantasy is something along the lines of a turbo-charged LandCruiser (all axles intact), cheap fuel and an off-road caravan. Although at the moment I just have a station wagon and a sleeping bag … But I'll get there eventually. As I said, anything is possible if you want it badly enough.

ACKNOWLEDGEMENTS

IN THE TWO YEARS IT'S TAKEN TO GET THIS book ready to publish I have had the support of many different people.

First of all, I have to thank the people who read about my crazy life in the Northern Territory on my blog kelsgonebush. com and encouraged me to turn my posts into something bigger. In particular, Andrea Jack, Buddy Wait, Al Zimdahl, Terri Samuels, Bianca Dart and Erica Counahan – your constant encouragement and belief in me helped me push through countless hours of editing and revision.

Robyn Flemming – thank you for reading through my first drafts and giving me some valuable advice about the publishing world!

Erin Grech – thank you for your suggestions in the first stages of my journey and helping me fine-tune my synopsis.

Phil O'Brien – my inspiration for kelsgonebush.com, thank you so much for not writing me off as a crazy fan! And I'm looking forward to a beer or two …

Thanks to my amazing agent, Virginia Lloyd, for taking a chance on me. Your guidance and encouragement – as well as your expert copy-editing skills – during the first major editing process was invaluable and I really felt like you were with me every step of the way. We did it!!

Sophie Hamley – I didn't think it could get any better than getting published but having my book personally looked after by someone as passionate about the Aussie outback as myself just about tops it off! Thank you for making the final stage of the publishing process so enjoyable – it really has been a pleasure .

Thanks to the rest of the fabulous team at Hachette: Chris Kunz, Jordan Weaver, Isabel Staas, Chris Sims, Ilse Scheepers, Sean Cotcher, Louise Sherwin-Stark, Justin Ractliffe and Fiona Hazard.

To my family, especially my mum, who has handled many a stressed-out phone call in the last two years and done a fantastic job of counselling me through the hard parts of writing a book – thank you!

My stepfather, Brendon: you never doubted this would happen.

My sister, Naomi, and brother, Todd – love you guys!

I couldn't forget my dad, who not only provided some hilarious material but passed on his love of the Aussie bush ... although camping with him was like camping with Russell Coight. Love ya, Dad.

Dave! You taught me so much – bush mechanics for a start. Thank you for taking me into your world of bush living and showing me parts of Australia I never knew existed. I also have to say thank you for helping me with facts and info for this book and the many times I made you proofread it.

Finally, thank you to my beautiful daughter, Marli Rose . You have inspired me to reach for the stars and I hope I will do the same for you! Love you, baby girl xx

About the Author

AFTER A COUPLE OF YEARS WORKING as a frazzled receptionist for one of the Gold Coast's largest Adult Entertainment agencies, Kellie decided to try her hand working as a 'skimpy' in mining towns around Australia. After a few months she relocated to Darwin where she worked as a skimpy barmaid and scored a regular gig on a Darwin FM radio station where, against all odds, she never swore on air. Kellie now lives with her daughter in Port Stephens, New South Wales. She has an entertainment blog www.kelsgonebush.com. This is her first book.

Spend more time in the Top End with

A collection of the funniest, craziest, wittiest, most memorable front pages from the *NT News*.

H hachette
AUSTRALIA

If you would like to find out more about
Hachette Australia, our authors, upcoming
events and new releases you can visit our website,
Facebook or follow us on Twitter:

hachette.com.au
twitter.com/HachetteAus
facebook.com/HachetteAustralia